W9-CHR-257

Phrase**Guide**

FRENCH

**With menu decoder, survival
guide and two-way dictionary**

Thomas Cook
Publishing

www.thomascookpublishing.com

Introduction......................5

The basics.....................................6

Grammar.....................................6
Basic conversation.....................8

Greetings...........................9

Meeting someone....................10
Small talk...............................10

Family.......................................11
Saying goodbye.......................12

Eating out......................13

The cuisines of France............14
National specialities................14
Lyon & Rhône-Alpes...............15
Provence & Côte d'Azur..........15
Alsace....................................16
The Alps.................................16
Brittany..................................17

Wine, beer & spirits.................17
Snacks & refreshments...........19
Vegetarians & special
requirements...........................19
Children...................................20
Menu decoder..........................21

Shopping.........................29

Essentials...............................30
Local specialities....................31
Popular things to buy..............31

Clothes & shoes......................32
Where to shop.........................35
Food & markets.......................36

Getting around...............37

Arrival....................................38
Customs.................................38
Car hire..................................39
On the road............................40

Directions................................40
Public transport.......................41
Taxis.......................................42
Tours.......................................42

Accommodation..............43

Types of accommodation........44
Reservations..........................44
Room types............................45
Prices....................................46

Special requests.....................47
Checking in & out....................48
Camping..................................48

Survival guide..................49

Money & banks........................50
Post office.............................51
Telecoms..............................52
Internet................................53
Chemist................................54

Children..................................55
Travellers with disabilities.......56
Repairs & cleaning...................57
Tourist information.........,.........58

Emergencies.....................59

Medical.................................60
Dentist.................................60
Crime...................................61
Lost property...........................61

Breakdowns.............................61
Problems with the
authorities................................62

Dictionary.......................63

English to French....................64

French to English....................79

Quick reference................95

Numbers....................................95
Weights & measures.................96

Days & time..................................96
Clothes size converter.............96

How to use this guide

The ten chapters in this guide are colour-coded to help you find what you're looking for. These colours are used on the tabs of the pages and in the contents on the opposite page and above.

For quick reference, you'll find some basic expressions on the inside front cover and essential emergency phrases on the inside back cover. There is also a handy reference section for numbers, measurements and clothes sizes at the back of the guide.

Front cover photography © Franck Dunouau / www.photolibrary.com
Cover design/artwork by Sharon Edwards
Photos: Peter Hellebrand (p9), Chloe Merle (p23), Adam Lambert-
Gorwyn (p28), Peter Russell (p32) and Bas Driessen (p59).

Produced by The Content Works Ltd
www.thecontentworks.com
Design concept: Mike Wade
Layout: Tika Stefano
Text: Nance Cooper
Editing: Aude Pasquier & Amanda Castleman
Proofing: Wendy Janes
Project editor: Begoña Juarros
Management: Lisa Plumridge & Rik Mulder

Published by Thomas Cook Publishing
A division of Thomas Cook Tour Operations Limited
PO Box 227, Unit 18, Coningsby Road
Peterborough PE3 8SB, United Kingdom
Company Registration Nº 1450464 England
email: books@thomascook.com
www.thomascookpublishing.com
+ 44 (0)1733 416477

ISBN-13: 978-1-84157-670-1

First edition © 2007 Thomas Cook Publishing
Text © 2007 Thomas Cook Publishing

Project Editor: Kelly Pipes
Production/DTP: Steven Collins

Printed and bound in Italy by Printer Trento

Introduction

French is a graceful language and the source of great pride for its native speakers. Less direct than English, the French will often use more words to describe something than a Brit would. It can be subtle. As Mark Twain remarked, it is especially suited "for the conveying of exquisitely nice shades of meaning". This should not put you off, however. The following introduction to this romantic language along with just a dash of charm will get you far.

Memorizing even a few phrases will greatly improve your travel experience. Simple statements – like **s'il vous plaît** (please) and **merci** (thank you) – demonstrate good intentions, which carry a lot of weight in such a proud, courtesy-conscious society. So don't be shy: **parlez français**!

Introduction

French is derived from Latin and a great many of its words have a clear Latin root. This can make it relatively easy to figure out the meaning of a word when confronted with it for the first time. If you think that you recognise the root of the word, you're probably right.

Regional accents are used in some parts but there is a standard pronunciation, a "neutral" French, which is the one taught in schools and which all educated French people speak, regardless of their provenance. This is also the French that is taught in schools in England. English natives can find it hard to master this correct French pronunciation, simply because the French use sounds that the English do not. However, there are a couple of tricks that can soon remedy this.

What's painful to the French ear when an English-speaker attempts to speak their language is the pronunciation of the letter "r". The French growl their "r"s. Practicing a 'grrrr' will help.

The vowels sound different, too: the French speak more from the front of their mouths, hence the famous French pout when they're talking. Try pouting a little when pronouncing the words and you may be surprised at how much more French you suddenly sound.

Grammar

Words in French have gender, not only people, but objects too. If they are masculine you use "un" (uhn) or "le" (luh), if they are feminine you use "une" (oon) or "la" (lah). There is no hard and fast rule for gender application, so the best thing is to pick it up as you go along.

French sentence structure is not drastically different from that in English. You will notice some inversion of word order (e.g. "the intelligent woman" will become "**la femme intelligente**", with the

Courtesy

Courtesy in language is a measure of class in France. Don't be afraid of being "over-courteous". It will be appreciated and you will be treated all the better for it.

adjective usually placed after the noun), but any mistakes you make will be nothing that a French person won't be able to understand.

In a normal sentence, the pronoun will be placed before the verb. The ending of a verb indicates when the action is taking place; **(Je) souhaite** means "I wish", while **(Je) souhaiterai** is "I will wish". A casual visitor doesn't need to memorize all the possibilities, just understand why a word can change from phrase to phrase.

Here's the most basic way to express an idea happening now. Take the infinitive – the "to X" form listed in the dictionary – and lop off the last two letters:

	souhait-er to wish	**fin-ir** to finish	**vend-re** to sell

Now add the appropriate ending:

je I	**souhait-e** wish	**fin-is** finish	**vend-s** sell
tu you	**souhait-es** wish	**fin-is** finish	**vend-s** sell
il, elle, on He/She	**souhait-e** wishes	**fin-it** finishes	**vend** sells
nous We	**souhait-ons** wish	**fin-issons** finish	**vend-ons** sell
vous You	**souhait-ez** wish	**fin-issez** finish	**vend-ez** sell
ils, elles They	**souhait-ent** wish	**fin-issent** finish	**vend-ent** sell

The French are excessively keen on courtesy, and correct phrasing can be a minefield, even for a seasoned French speaker. Something that would be perfectly acceptable in English can come across as rude or pushy in French. Your best weapon here is a smile and a friendly attitude. It is seen as more polite to speak French and make mistakes than to give up and just use English. The French will generally be more patient with someone who's making the effort. They'll also find it hard to resist correcting you. This is a friendly gesture, though: they're very proud of their language and want to help you speak it better. One of the most important rules of courtesy is the "**vouvoiement**" (the rule of referring to people using the polite term of "**vous**" as opposed to "**tu**"). This must be used at all times when talking to adults unless otherwise agreed. Use it when talking to someone you don't know, that you've just met or with whom you share a non-friendship or non-familial bond, such as a work colleague. Do not use it when talking to children, however. If in doubt, use "**vous**", you will soon be told if it is not necessary and your courtesy will be appreciated nonetheless.

Basic conversation

English	French	Pronunciation
Hello	**Bonjour**	*bonzhoor*
Goodbye	**Au revoir**	*oh revwaar*
Yes	**Oui**	*wee*
No	**Non**	*nohn*
Please	**S'il vous plait**	*seel voo play*
Thank you	**Merci**	*mairsee*
You're welcome	**Je vous en prie**	*zhe voos ohn pree*
Sorry	**Excusez-moi**	*exkoozay mwa*
Excuse me (apology)	**Je suis désolé**	*zhe swee dayzolay*
Excuse me (to get attention)	**Excusez-moi**	*exkoozay mwa*
Excuse me (to get past)	**Excusez-moi**	*exkoozay mwa*
Do you speak English?	**Parlez-vous anglais?**	*parlay-voo ohnglay?*
I don't speak French	**Je ne parle pas français**	*zhe nuh parl pa fronsay*
I speak a little French	**Je parle un peu français**	*zhe parl uhn puh fronsay*
What?	**Quoi?**	*kwa?*
I understand	**Je comprends**	*zhuh komprohn*
I don't understand	**Je ne comprends pas**	*zhe nuh komprohn-par*
Do you understand?	**Vous comprenez?**	*voo compruhnay?*
I don't know	**Je ne sais pas**	*zhe nuh sey pah*
I can't	**Je ne peux pas**	*zhe nuh puh pah*
Can you ... please?	**Pouvez-vous ... s'il vous plaît?**	*poovay-voo ... seel voo play?*
- speak more slowly	**-parler plus lentement**	*-parlay ploo lohntamohn*
- repeat that	**-répéter**	*-reppaytay*

8

Greetings

Courtesy is key in France, so prepare
for effusive greetings and air-kisses
(three to five at last count). Nod politely
when passing a stranger on the street
or while sharing a lift, especially if you
are the only two people present. Finally,
forget all the grim tales about Parisians
snubbing poor French accents: almost
any attempt is welcome these days.

Conversational etiquette is highly
regarded by the French. The stylish
raise it to an art form, the practical
consider it a pleasant way of
punctuating the day; either way,
courtesy is of paramount importance
when encountering strangers. Simply
remember the key theme of French
etiquette: respect.

Meeting someone

Hello	**Bonjour**	*bohnzhoor*
Hi	**Salut**	*saloo*
Good morning	**Bonjour**	*bohnzhoor*
Good afternoon	**Bonjour**	*bohnzhoor*
Good evening	**Bonsoir**	*bohnswar*
Sir/Mr	**Monsieur**	*muhsseyuh*
Madam/Mrs	**Madame**	*madam*
Miss	**Mademoiselle**	*maduhmwasel*
How are you?	**Comment allez-vous?**	*kohmohnt allay-voo?*
Fine, thank you	**Très bien, merci**	*trey byen mairsee*
And you?	**Et vous?**	*ay voo?*
Very well	**Très bien**	*trey byen*
Not very well	**Pas très bien**	*pa trey byen*

Goodnight versus sleep tight
Only say **bonne nuit** if you know the person well
enough to wish them a good night's sleep. Otherwise,
for example when leaving a party or dinner, **bonne
soirée** – have a good evening – is the correct form.

Small talk

My name is...	**Je m'appelle...**	*zhuh mapel...*
What's your name?	**Comment vous appelez-vous?**	*kohmohn voos apuh-lay-voo?*
I'm pleased to meet you	**Je suis ravi de faire votre connaissance**	*zhuh swee ravee duh fair vohtruh konayssohnce*
Where are you from?	**D'où venez-vous?**	*doo vuhnay-voo?*

I am from Britain	**Je viens de Grande Bretagne**	*zhuh vyen duh grohnd bruhtanyuh*
Do you live here?	**Habitez-vous ici?**	*abeetay-voo eecee?*
This is a great...	**C'est... génial/e**	*say...zhaynyal*
- country	**- un pays**	*- uhn payee*
- city/town	**- une ville**	*- oon veel*
I am staying at...	**Je suis au/à la...**	*zhuh swee oh/ah la...*
I'm just here for the day	**Je suis ici pour une journée seulement**	*zhuh swees eecee poor oon zhournay suhluhmohn*
I'm in...for	**Je suis à...pour**	*zhuh swees ah...poor*
- a weekend	**- un week-end**	*- uhn weekend*
- a week	**- une semaine**	*- oon suhmen*
How old are you?	**Quel âge avez-vous?**	*kel arzh avay-voo?*
I'm... years old	**J'ai...ans**	*jay...ohn*

Family

This is my...	**Voici...**	*vwacee...*
- husband	**- mon mari**	*- mohn maree*
- wife	**- ma femme**	*- mah fam*
- partner	**- mon conjoint**	*- mohn kohnzhoohen*
- boyfriend/ girlfriend	**- mon petit ami/ma petite amie**	*- mohn puhtee amee/mah puteet amee*
I have a...	**J'ai...**	*zhay...*
- son	**- un garçon**	*- uhn garsohn*
- daughter	**- une fille**	*- oon feeyuh*
- grandson	**- un petit-fils**	*- uhn puhtee-feese*
- granddaughter	**- une petite-fille**	*- oon puhteet-feeyuh*
Do you have...	**Avez-vous...**	*avay-voo...*
- children?	**- des enfants?**	*- dey ohnfohn?*
- grandchildren?	**- des petits-enfants?**	*- dey puhtees-ohnfohn?*
I don't have children	**Je n'ai pas d'enfants**	*zhuh nay pa dohn-fohn*
Are you married?	**Etes-vous marié/e?**	*ett-voo marreyay?*

I'm...	Je suis...	*zhuh swee...*
- single	- célibataire	*- selleebatair*
- married	- marié/e	*- marreeyay*
- divorced	- divorcé/e	*- deevorsay*
- a widow/widower	- veuve/veuf	*- vuhv/vuhf*

Saying goodbye

Goodbye	Au revoir	*oh ruhvwar*
Good evening	Bonne soirée	*bon swaray*
Goodnight	Bonne nuit	*bon nwee*
Sleep well	Dormez bien	*dormay byen*
See you later	A plus tard	*ah ploo tar*
Have a good trip	Bon voyage	*bohn vwayazh*
It was nice meeting you	Cela m'a fait plaisir de vous rencontrer	*suhlah m'ah fay pleyseer duh voo rohnkontrey*
All the best	Je vous souhaite plein de bonheur	*zhuh voo sooet plahn duh bonuhr*
Have fun	Amusez-vous bien	*amoozay-voo byen*
Good luck	Bonne chance pour tout	*bonn shohnce poor too*
Keep in touch	Nous restons en contact	*noo resthon ohn kontakt*
My address is...	Mon adresse est...	*mohn adress ay...*
What's your...	Quel(le) est votre...	*kel ay vohtruh...*
- address?	- adresse?	*- adress?*
- email?	- adresse email?	*- adress ee-mell?*
- telephone number?	- numéro de téléphone?	*- noomayro duh tey-leyfohn*

Once more, with feeling

The intense hellos and goodbyes may sound over the top to a Brit. Unstiffen your lip and run with it. You'll connect more with the locals.

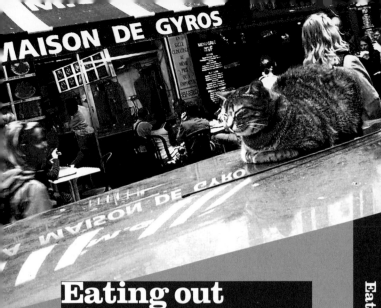

Eating out

France is the birthplace of restaurants, the word itself originating in the French word meaning "to restore". Places to eat here display a very ordered approach towards service, with members of staff trained in and focused on one role. This may result in your being served by four different people over the course of one meal.

Menu favourites include **coq au vin** (chicken cooked in wine), **moules frites** (garlic and herb mussels served with chips) and **tarte tatin** (upside down apple tart). Yet each region fiercely defends its culinary style, favourite ingredients and signature dishes.

Bon appétit!

Introduction

Cafés are the pubs of France. They all serve alcohol and often double as tobacconists. Here locals gather to chitchat and, of course, chain-smoke. Ignore the gatecrashing sensation; a courteous visitor is soon adopted. Then you can join Junior propping up the bar – sipping lemonade, mind – because cafés welcome all ages. Lunch is the main meal, so expect generous portions. Happily, these are much cheaper than the usual fare.

I'd like...	**J'aimerais...**	_jemmaray..._
- a table for two	**- une table pour deux**	_- oon tabluh poor duh_
- a sandwich	**- un sandwich**	_- uhn sohndweech_
- a coffee	**- un café**	_- uhn kafa_
- a tea (with milk)	**- un thé (au lait)**	_- uhn tay (oh lay)_
Do you have a menu in English?	**Avez-vous un menu en anglais?**	_avay-voo uhn muh-noo ohn ohnglay?_
The bill, please	**L'addition, s'il vous plaît**	_lahdeesion, seel voo play_

You may hear...

Fumeur ou non-fumeur	_foomuhr oo nohn-foomuhr_	Smoking or non-smoking?
Que prendrez-vous?	_kuh prohndrey-voo?_	What are you going to have?

The cuisines of France

National specialities

The French excel at cooking meat and fish, and bringing out any ingredient's best. Chefs showcase local grub whenever possible – part of the Slow Food ethos – and dishes tend to be elegant, yet rich.

Signature dishes
(see the Menu decoder for more dishes)

Steak au poivre	_stek oh pwavruh_	Steak with a pepper-corn crust
Blanquette de veau	_blohnket duh voh_	White veal stew, often served with potatoes
Huîtres	_weetruh_	Oysters
Soufflé	_sooflay_	Fluffy baked dessert

Lyon & Rhône-Alpes

Lyon is the heartland of the nation's cuisine, producing many of France's most revered dishes. The full, rich flavours embrace local produce, such as **quenelles**, tripe and poultry.

Lyon's share
Lyon is the nation's true culinary capital, ideally placed between two exquisite wine regions: Beaujolais and Côtes du Rhône.

Signature dishes

(see the Menu decoder for more dishes)

Coq au vin	_kok oh vahn_	Chicken cooked with wine
Pot-au-feu	_poht oh fuhr_	Beef pot roast
Quenelles	_kuhnell_	Ground patty made with white meat or fish
Volaille de Bresse	_vohlie duh Bress_	Tender Bresse poultry
Andouillette	_ohndooyett_	Tripe Lyon style

Provence & Côte d'Azur

This area's climate has distinctive warmth, echoed in its food. Dishes exhibit lots of vivid colour and sometimes spiciness too. Fish and seafood feature strongly and are always a good bet.

Signature dishes

(see the Menu decoder for more dishes)

Bouillabaisse	_booyabayss_	Mixed fish stew
Ratatouille	_ratatooyuh_	Vegetable stew
Pissaladière	_peessaladyair_	Onion pie with anchovy paste
Socca	_sohkka_	Hot chickpea pancake

15

| Salade Niçoise | sa<u>lad</u> nee<u>swahs</u> | Vegetable, egg and tuna salad |

Alsace

Alsace lies near Germany and Switzerland, and its cuisine very much reflects this. Light, it is not. Rather it weighs in on the generous and soul-warming side. Pork is popular, most often with roast potatoes and dumplings, all washed down with the region's famous beers or white wines.

Signature dishes
(see the Menu decoder for more dishes)

Tarte flambée	tart floh<u>mbay</u>	Pizza with crème fraîche, bacon and onions
Baeckeoffe	bay<u>koff</u>	Sliced potatoes sealed in a crust
Choucroute garnie	shoo<u>kroot</u> gar<u>nee</u>	Sour cabbage with sausages
Spatzle	<u>spatz</u>el	Small noodles served with meat
Kouglof	<u>koog</u>lof	Sweet cake

Tarte Flambée
Farmers originally cooked **tarte flambée** to test the heat of their ovens: the ideal temperature would bake one in two minutes. Traditional Alsatian restaurants keep these pies coming until you ask them to stop.

The Alps
Alpine specialties are designed for hungry skiers, larding on the cheese, potatoes, wine and more cheese. As a result, this cuisine is one of the tastiest in France. Bring an appetite; they won't let you leave with one.

The meaning of Michelin
French Chef Bernard Loiseau took his life, rather than see his restaurant Côte d'Or lose its Michelin star ranking.

Signature dishes
(see the Menu decoder for more dishes)

Raclette	*rak<u>lett</u>*	Melted cheese with potatoes and ham
Fondue Savoyarde	*fohn<u>doo</u> savwa<u>yard</u>*	Cheese and white wine fondue
Tartiflette	*tartee<u>flett</u>*	Gratin with Reblochon cheese, cream and pork

Brittany

Though most famous for its alcoholic drinks, Brittany offers a robust, healthy variation on French cuisine. Seafood and wheat pancakes are standouts.

Signature dishes
(see the Menu decoder for more dishes)

Galettes Bretonnes	*gal<u>ett</u> bruhto<u>nn</u>*	Buckwheat pancakes with range of fillings
Kouign Amann	*kweehn a<u>mann</u>*	Butter and sugar pancake
Lambig	*lohm<u>beeg</u>*	Apple eau-de-vie
Chouchen	*shoo<u>shenn</u>*	Mead
Kir Breton	*keer bruh<u>tohn</u>*	Crème de cassis and cider

Wine, beer & spirits

France's winemaking tradition is much revered. Each region has its highlights from champagne in Champagne-Ardenne, to red wine in Aquitaine and beer in Alsace.

Signature dishes
(see the Menu decoder for more dishes)

Vin de pays...	*vahn duh payee...*	Wine from a specific region...
Beaujolais nouveau	*bohzholay noovo*	The year's Beaujolais, to be drunk immediately
Pastis	*pasteess*	Aniseed-flavoured **apéritif** drunk diluted in water
Limoncello	*leemonchello*	Originally Italian **digestif** made with lemons
Armagnac	*armanyak*	Older and rarer French brandy

Finding a good restaurant
Avoid eateries with touts or tourist menus. Ask a local **en route** to lunch for advice – or just follow behind.

Could I have...?	**Pourrais-je avoir...?**	*pooray-zhuh avwar...?*
- a beer	**- une bière**	*- oon byair*
- a glass/a bottle of white/red/ rosé wine	**- un verre/une bouteille de vin blanc/rouge/rosé**	*- uhn vair/oon bootayuh duh vahn blohn/roozhe/rosay*
- a glass/a bottle of champagne	**- une coupe/une bouteille de champagne**	*- oon koop/oon bootayuh duh shomparnyuh*
- a gin and tonic	**- un gin tonic**	*- uhn jeen toneek*

| - a rum and coke | - un rhum-coca/ Cuba Libre | - uhn rum koh<u>ka</u>/ kuba lee<u>bray</u> |
| - a whisky | - un whisky | - uhn wee<u>skee</u> |

Bad service
Protest shoddy service by tipping a single **cent**, just like the locals.

You may hear...

Que puis-je vous servir?	kuh <u>pwee</u>-zhuh voos sehr<u>vihr</u>?	What can I get you?
Comment l'aimeriez-vous?	ko<u>mohn</u> lemuhree<u>yay</u>-voo?	How would you like it?
Avec ou sans glaçons?	ah<u>vek</u> oo sohn glas<u>sohn</u>?	With or without ice?
Frais ou chambré?	freh oo sham<u>breh</u>?	Cold or room temperature?

Snacks & refreshments

Coffee is served black and, of course, fresh. Order **café-au-lait** for a milky blend, similar to **latté**. Tea options tend to be limited. The French enjoy pastries at breakfast, typically a **croissant** or a **pain-au-chocolat**.

Coffee	Café	ka<u>fay</u>
Coffee with milk	Café au lait	ka<u>fay</u> oh lay
Tea	Thé	tay
Herbal tea	Infusion	ahnfoo<u>sion</u>

Vegetarians & special requirements

I'm vegetarian	Je suis végétarien	zhuh swee vayjayta-ree<u>yahn</u>
I don't eat...	Je ne mange pas...	zhuh nuh <u>mohn</u>je pa...
- meat	- de viande	- duh vee<u>yohnd</u>
- fish	- de poisson	- duh pwas<u>sohn</u>

19

Could you cook something without meat in it?	**Pouvez-vous me préparer quelque chose sans viande?**	*poovay-voo muh prayparay kelkuhshows sohn veeyohnd?*
What's in this?	**Qu'y a t-il dedans?**	*kee yateel duhdohn?*
I'm allergic...	**Je suis allergique...**	*zhuh swees alairzheek...*
- to peanuts	**- à l'arachide**	*- ah l'arasheed*
- to wheat	**- au blé**	*- oh blay*
- to dairy products	**- aux produits laitiers**	*- oh prodwee laytyay*
- to nuts	**- aux noix**	*- oh nwa*

Smoking

The French smoke – and how! On request, some may stub out, say, if a child is present. Asking isn't socially graceful, however.

Children

Are children welcome?	**Les enfants sont-ils les bienvenus?**	*ley ohnfohn sohnt-eel ley byenvuhnoo?*
Do you have a children's menu?	**Avez-vous un menu enfant?**	*avay-voo uhn muhnoo ohnfohn?*
What dishes are good for children?	**Quels plats iraient pour les enfants?**	*kel pla ihray poor leys ohnfohn?*

Menu decoder

Essentials

Breakfast	**Petit déjeuner**	*puhtee dayjuhnay*
Lunch	**Déjeuner**	*dayjuhnay*
Dinner	**Dîner**	*deenay*
Cover charge	**Prix du couvert**	*pree do koovair*
VAT inclusive	**TVA incluse**	*tay vay ah ahnklooz*
Service included	**Service compris**	*sairveess compree*
Credit cards (not) accepted	**Nous (n') acceptons (pas) les cartes de crédit**	*noo (n) axeptohn (pa) ley kart duh krehdee*
First course	**Entrée**	*ahntray*
Second course	**Plat principal**	*plah prahceepahl*
Side dish	**Garniture**	*garneetoor*
Dessert	**Dessert**	*dayssair*
Dish of the day	**Plat du jour**	*plah doo zhoor*
House specials	**Spécialités de la maison**	*spaysialeetay duh lah maysohn*
Set menu	**Menu fixe**	*muhnoo feex*
A la carte menu	**Menu à la carte**	*muhnoo ah la kart*
Tourist menu	**Menu touriste**	*muhnoo tooreest*
Wine list	**Carte des vins**	*kart dey vahn*
Drinks menu	**Carte des boissons**	*kart dey bwasson*
Snack menu	**Carte des snacks**	*kart day snak*

Methods of preparation

Baked	**Cuit (au four)**	*kwee (oh foor)*
Boiled	**Bouilli**	*booyee*
Braised	**A l'étouffée**	*ah laytooffay*
Breaded	**Pané**	*panay*
Deep-fried	**Frit**	*free*
Fresh	**Frais**	*fray*
Fried	**Poêlé**	*pwaley*
Frozen	**Congelé**	*conjuhlay*
Grilled/broiled	**Grillé**	*greeyay*
Marinated	**Mariné**	*mareenay*
Mashed	**Ecrasé / en purée**	*Eycrasey / ohn puray*

Fast food

The French openly despise fast-food chains but the younger generation has embraced them. Be prepared for a longer wait than you're used to; the only thing "fast" about this food is the name.

Poached	**Poché**	*poshey*
Raw	**Cru**	*cru*
Roasted	**Rôti**	*rotee*
Salty	**Salé**	*saley*
Sautéed	**Sauté**	*sohtay*
Smoked	**Fumé**	*fumay*
Spicy (flavour)	**Epicé**	*epeessay*
Spicy (hot)	**Relevé**	*rehlevay*
Steamed	**A la vapeur**	*ah la vapuhr*
Stewed	**En daube**	*ahn dohbe*
Stuffed	**Fourré**	*fooray*
Sweet	**Sucré**	*sukray*
Rare	**Saignant**	*saynyan*
Medium	**A point**	*ah pwan*
Well done	**Bien cuit**	*byen kwee*

Common food items

Beef	**Boeuf**	*buhf*
Chicken	**Poulet**	*pooley*
Fish	**Poisson**	*pwassohn*
Lamb	**Agneau**	*anyoh*
Pork	**Porc**	*pore*
Seafood	**Fruits de mer**	*frewee deh mair*
Turkey	**Dinde**	*dahnd*
Beans	**Haricots**	*areekoh*
Cheese	**Fromage**	*frohmazhe*
Eggs	**Oeufs**	*uhf*
Lentils	**Lentilles**	*lohnteey*
Pasta/noodles	**Pâtes/nouilles**	*pat/nooyuh*
Rice	**Riz**	*ree*
Tuna	**Thon**	*tohn*
Cabbage	**Chou**	*shoo*
Carrots	**Carottes**	*carott*
Cucumber	**Concombre**	*concombruh*
Garlic	**Ail**	*i*
Mushrooms	**Champignons**	*shompeenyon*
Olives	**Olives**	*ohleev*
Onion	**Oignon**	*onyohn*
Potato	**Pomme de terre**	*pom deh tair*
Red/green pepper	**Poivron rouge/vert**	*pwavrohn roozh/vair*
Tomato	**Tomate**	*tohmat*
Vegetables	**Légumes**	*laygum*
Bread	**Pain**	*pahn*
Oil	**Huile**	*weel*
Pepper	**Poivre**	*pwavruh*
Salt	**Sel**	*sell*
Vinegar	**Vinaigre**	*veenaygruh*
Cake	**Gâteau**	*gatoh*
Cereals	**Céréales**	*sayrayal*
Cream	**Crème**	*krem*
Fruit	**Fruit**	*frewee*
Ice-cream	**Glace / Crème glacée**	*glass/krem glassey*
Milk	**Lait**	*lay*

Tart	**Tarte**	*tahrt*

Popular sauces

Béarnaise	*bairnayz*	Thick, creamy butter sauce
Au poivre	*oh pwavruh*	Creamy pepper sauce
Vinaigrette	*veenaygrett*	Fragrant salad dressing made with oil, vinegar and mustard
Crème de champignons	*krem duh shom-peenyon*	Creamy mushroom sauce
Mayonnaise	*my-onez*	Mayonnaise, often eaten with chips
Ketchup	*ketchup*	Tomato ketchup
Moutarde	*mootard*	Mustard
Moutarde à l'ancienne	*mootard ah lahn-syenn*	Old-style mustard with mustard seeds

First course dishes

Melon et Jambon de Parme	*muhlon ay zhom-bon duh parm*	Melon with Parma ham
Salade de chèvre chaud	*salad duh shevryh showd*	Warm goat's cheese salad
Huîtres	*weetruh*	Raw oysters

Mussels from Brussels
The French often put mayonnaise on their chips, Belgian-style. Another approach which the French have borrowed from the Belgians is serving mussels with chips.

Avoiding the traps

Avoiding tourist traps can be as simple as asking a local for their recommendations, or skirting restaurants that only post menus in English outside.

Soupe à l'oignon	*soop ah lonyohn*	Onion soup
Tomates mozzarella	*tohmat mozzarella*	Tomato, mozzarella and basil
Carpaccio de boeuf	*carpachio duh buhf*	Thinly sliced raw beef
Salade mixte	*salad meext*	Mixed salad leaves
Terrine	*taireen*	Savoury pâté
Tomates farcies	*tohmat farsee*	Stuffed tomatoes
Soufflé au fromage	*sooflay oh fromazh*	Cheese soufflé
Gratinée de coquilles St Jacques	*grateenay duh kokee San Zhak*	Gratinéed scallops
Mousse de saumon	*mooss duh sohmohn*	Salmon mousse
Salade d'endives	*salad dohndeev*	Endive salad
Quiche Lorraine	*keesh Lorren*	Ham and cheese quiche
Soupe d'asperges	*soop daspairzh*	Asparagus soup
Vichyssoise	*veesheeswas*	Cold vegetable soup

Second course dishes

Steak frites	*stek feet*	Steak and chips
Steak au poivre	*stek oh pwavruh*	Steak in a pepper crust
Poulet rôti	*pooley rohtee*	Roast chicken

Cordon Bleu	*kordohn bluh*	Cheese and ham filled chicken
Pavé d'espadon	*pavay desspadon*	Swordfish steak
Pavé de saumon	*pavay duh sohmohn*	Salmon steak
Moules frites	*mool freet*	Garlic and herb mussels with chips
Sauté de volaille	*sohtay duh vohlie*	Sautéed chicken
Escalope panée	*esscalop panay*	Breaded chicken escalope
Steak tartare	*stek tartar*	Seasoned raw minced beef
Raviolis aux cèpes	*raviolee oh sep*	Mushroom ravioli
Filet mignon	*feelay meenyon*	Pork filet mignon
Emincé de volaille	*aymahnsay duh voh-lie*	Thinly sliced chicken fillet
Terrine de saumon aux épinards	*taireen duh sohmohn ohz epeenar*	Salmon and spinach terrine
Fricassée de mer	*freekassay duh mair*	Mixed fish and scallops
Blanquette de veau	*blanket duh voh*	Veal stew
Boeuf Bourguignon	*buhf boorg-eenyon*	Beef stew
Lapin à la moutarde	*lahpahn ah la mootard*	Rabbit in mustard sauce

Side dishes

Salade verte	*salad vairt*	Green salad
Gratin de pommes de terre	*gratahn duh pom deh tair*	Potato gratin
Frites	*freet*	French fries
Pommes de terre sautées	*pom duh tair sohtay*	Sautéed potatoes
Légumes frais cuits au four	*laygoom fray kwee oh foor*	Oven-baked fresh vegetables
Courgettes sautées à l'ail	*koorjett sohtay ah lie*	Sautéed courgettes with garlic
Haricots verts	*areekoh vair*	Green beans
Riz	*ree*	Rice
Carottes rapées	*carott rapey*	Grated carrot
Epinards à la crème	*epeenar ah la krem*	Spinach cooked with cream
Julienne de légumes	*zhoolyenn duh laygoom*	Thinly shredded vegetables

Tapenade	*tapuh<u>nad</u>*	Olive paste
Taboulé	*tahboo<u>lay</u>*	Cracked wheat salad

Desserts

Crème brûlée	*krem broo<u>lay</u>*	Pudding with caramel crust
Crème caramel	*krem cara<u>mel</u>*	Custard pudding with caramel
Soufflé	*soo<u>flay</u>*	Fluffy baked pudding
Fondant au chocolat	*fon<u>dohn</u> oh showkoh<u>la</u>*	Cake with melted chocolate centre
Tarte aux pommes	*tahrt oh pom*	Sliced apple tart
Tarte au citron	*tahrt oh see<u>tron</u>*	Lemon cream tart
Salade de fruits	*salad duh frewee*	Fruit salad
Poire Belle-Hélène	*pwar bell-eh<u>lehn</u>*	Pears with chocolate
Profiteroles	*profeetuh<u>roll</u>*	Choux pastry with chocolate sauce
Gratin de fruits rouges	*gra<u>tahn</u> duh fre-wee roozh*	Sugar-gratinéd berries
Congolais	*kongoh<u>lay</u>*	Coconut biscuits
Pain d'épice	*pahn deh<u>peess</u>*	Spiced honey cake
Fraisier	*frayz<u>yay</u>*	Strawberry cake
Madeleines	*mahduh<u>len</u>*	Small sweet cakes

Drinks

Vin rouge	*vahn roozh*	Red wine
Vin blanc	*vahn blahn*	White wine
Rosé	*ro<u>say</u>*	Rosé wine
Bière	*byair*	Beer
Blonde	*blohnd*	Lager
Pression	*preh<u>ssyon</u>*	Draught beer
Eau minérale	*oh meenay<u>ral</u>*	Mineral water
Soda	*sodah*	Fizzy drink
Jus d'orange	*joo do<u>rahnj</u>*	Orange juice
Coca	*koh<u>kah</u>*	Coca-cola
Limonade	*leemoh<u>nad</u>*	Lemonade
Pastis	*pas<u>teess</u>*	Aniseed liqueur
Champagne	*shompan*	Champagne

Snacks

Croque-monsieur	*croe nuhsseyuh*	Grilled ham and cheese sandwich
Panini	*panee<u>nee</u>*	Grilled sandwich

Sandwich jambon-fromage (Parisien)	*sohndweech zhombohn-fromazh (pareesiehn)*	Ham and cheese sandwich
Feuilleté de chèvre	*fuhyuhtay duh chehvruh*	Pastry with goat's cheese
Feuilleté saucisse	*fuhyuhtay sohseess*	Delicate sausage roll
Vol-au-vent	*vol-oh-vohn*	Puff pastry with filling
Crudités variées	*kroodeetay varyay*	Mixed fresh vegetables
Beignets	*baynyay*	Doughnuts
Crêpe salée	*krep salay*	Pancake with savoury filling
Crêpe sucrée	*krep sookray*	Pancake with sweet filling
Camembert fondue	*kamombair fondoo*	Melted Camembert cheese
Brioche	*breeyosh*	Sweet bread

Snacks

Bakeries rather than supermarkets are where the French go to pick up a quick sandwich for lunch. These sandwiches will have been made the same day though the baker probably won't have time to make you one on the spot.

Shopping

France offers a large number of delights for shopaholics. For one thing, it has a very active crafts industry, with many original products and unique works of art. The French would certainly claim that their regional food specialities are also the work of craftsmen and women and you'll be hard pressed to find delicacies produced with as much care and attention elsewhere. This is a matter of national pride. You'll find a tremendous variety of wares on offer and great global brands stand side by side with small specialist shops. There really is something for everyone here.

Essentials

Where can I buy...?	**Où puis-je acheter...?**	*oo pwee-zhuh ashuhtay...?*
I'd like to buy...	**J'aimerais acheter...**	*jemmaray ashuhtay...*
Do you have...?	**Auriez-vous...?**	*oreeyay voo...?*
I'd like this	**J'aimerais ceci**	*jemmaray suhsee*
I'd prefer...	**Je préférerais...**	*zhuh preyfairuhray...*
Could you show me...?	**Pourriez-vous me montrer...?**	*pooreeyay-voo muh mohntrey...?*
I'm just looking, thanks	**Je regarde, merci**	*zhuh ruhgard, mairsee*
How much is it?	**Combien est-ce que ça coûte?**	*kombyen ess kuh sa koot?*
Could you write down the price?	**Pourriez-vous m'écrire le prix?**	*pooreeyay-voo maykreer luh pree?*
Do you have any items on sale?	**Avez-vous des articles soldés?**	*avay-voo deyz arteekluh soldey?*
Could I have a discount?	**Pourrais-je avoir une réduction?**	*pooray-zhuh avwar oon raydooksion?*
Nothing else, thanks	**Rien d'autre, merci**	*ryen dohtr, mairsee*
Do you accept credit cards?	**Acceptez-vous les cartes de crédit?**	*acceptay-voo ley kart duh kreydee?*

The daily chat with the baker

Going to the baker in the morning is a social occasion and a good opportunity to chat with the locals and ask questions. Greet the baker and be prepared to have a full-blown conversation with him and anyone else who enters the bakery.

It's a present, could I have it wrapped, please?	C'est pour un cadeau. Pouvez-vous me faire un paquet cadeau, s'il vous plaît?	*sey poor uhn kadoh. poovay-voo muh fair uhn pakay kadoh, seel voo play?*
Could you post it to...?	Pourriez-vous l'envoyer à...?	*pooreeyay-voo lohn-vwayay ah...?*
Can I exchange it?	Je pourrais faire un échange?	*zhuh pooray fayr uhn ayshanzh?*
I'd like to return this	J'aimerais faire un échange	*jemmaray fayr uhn ayshanzh*
I'd like a refund	J'aimerais me faire rembourser	*jemmaray meh fayr rahmboorsay*

Local specialities

France is excessively proud of its history of craftsmanship, and every region will have a mind-blowing array of unique special products. A good idea is to keep an eye open if you're on the road. You'll notice signposts showing the way to tiny, out-of-the-way farms and houses where locals produce and sell their own handiwork. They will also take these products to the periodic markets in their nearest town, so ask a local to find out when the dates for these markets are. Haggling is often possible but isn't the norm.

Can you recommend a shop selling local specialities?	Pouvez-vous me recommander un magasin vendant les spécialités locales?	*poovay-voo muh ruh-cohmmohnday uhn magasahn vohndohn ley speseeyaleetay lohkal?*
What should I buy from here?	Que devrais-je acheter d'ici?	*kuh devray-zhuh ashuhtay deesee?*
Is...(leather) good quality?	(Le cuir)...est-il de bonne qualité?	*(luh kweer)...ayt-eel duh bonn kaleetay?*
Is it hand made?	Est-ce que c'est fait à la main?	*esskuh say fey ah la mahn?*
Do you make it to measure?	Le fabriquez-vous sur mesure?	*luh fabreekay-voo sooer muhsoor?*
Can I order one?	Puis-je en commander un?	*pwee-zhuh ohn cohmohnday uhn?*

Popular things to buy

| La lavande | *la lavohnde* | Lavender |
| De la poterie | *duh la pohtcree* | Pottery |

Les herbes de provence	*leyz airbuh duh prohvohnce*	Provencal herbs
Le fromage de chèvre	*luh frohmazh duh shehvr*	Goat's cheese
Le camembert	*luh camohmbair*	Camembert cheese
Le vin rouge/ blanc	*luh van roozhe/ blohn*	Red/white wine
Le champagne	*luh shohmpanyuh*	Champagne
Le rosé	*luh rohsay*	Rosé wine
Le parfum	*luh parfuhn*	Perfume
Les peintures	*ley pahntur*	Paintings
Les vêtements de mode/haute couture	*ley vetmohn duh mohd/ ot kootur*	Fashion/couture clothing
Les pâtisseries	*ley pateessuhree*	Pastries
Les truffes	*ley truf*	Truffles
Le foie gras	*luh fwa gra*	Foie Gras

Sunday shopping

Most shops in France are closed on Sundays, sometimes Saturday afternoons as well. You will also find that many close for an hour or two at lunchtime during the week.

Clothes & shoes

Clothing is generally less expensive in France than in the UK, whether you're visiting a prestigious shopping gallery like the "Galeries Lafayette" in Paris or a tiny shop in Provence. France is of course famous for its fashion industry and you'll find a vast array of styles on offer. Remember to ask whether the shop accepts returns; some will give exchanges but getting a reimbursement can be tricky.

Where is the... department?	**Où se trouve le rayon des...**	*oo suh troove luh rayohn duh...*
- clothes	**- vêtements?**	*- vetmohn?*

- shoe	**- chaussures?**	- _shohssur?_
- women's	**- femmes?**	- _fam?_
- men's	**- hommes?**	- _om?_
- children's	**- enfants?**	- _ohnfohn?_

I'm looking for...	**Je cherche...**	_zhe shairsh..._
- a skirt	**- une jupe**	- _oon zhoop_
- trousers	**- un pantalon**	- _uhn pohntalohn_
- a top	**- un haut**	- _uhn oh_
- a jacket	**- une veste**	- _oon vest_
- a T-shirt	**- un tee-shirt**	- _uhn tee-shurt_
- jeans	**- un jeans**	- _uhn jean_
- shoes	**- des chaussures**	- _dey shohssur_
- underwear	**- des sous-vêtements**	- _dey soo-vetmohn_

Can I try it on?	**Puis-je l'essayer?**	_pwee-zhe lessayay?_
What size is it?	**Quelle taille fait-il?**	_kel tie fetteel?_
My size is...	**Je fais du...**	_zhe fay duh..._
- small	**- S**	- _ayss_
- medium	**- M**	- _aym_
- large	**- L**	- _ayll_

(see clothes size converter on p.96 for full range of sizes)

| Where is the changing room? | **Où sont les cabines d'essayage?** | _oo sohn ley kabeen d ayssayazh?_ |

| It doesn't fit | **Ce n'est pas la bonne taille** | _suh ney pa la bonn tie_ |
| It doesn't suit me | **Ça ne me va pas** | _sa nuh muh va pa_ |

Gift wrapping

Many shops will offer to wrap your purchases if you tell them that they are gifts. Most do not charge for this service but expect to pay about EUR 2 to those who do.

33

Do you have a... size?	**Avez-vous une taille...**	*avay-voo oon tie...*
- bigger	**- plus grande?**	*- ploo grohnd?*
- smaller	**- plus petite?**	*- ploo puhteet?*
Do you have it/them in...	**Vous l'avez en...**	*voo l'avay ohn...*
- black?	**- noir?**	*- nwar?*
- white?	**- blanc?**	*- blohn?*
- blue?	**- bleu?**	*- blur?*
- green?	**- vert?**	*- vair?*
- red?	**- rouge?**	*- roozhe?*
I'm going to leave it/them	**Je vais le/les laisser**	*zhe vey luh/ley lessey*
I'll take it / them	**Je vais le/les prendre**	*zhe vey luh/ley prohndruh*

At the till

The French are very sociable at work. This is lovely until you get stuck in a queue behind a customer who knows the shop assistant. Expect a ten-minute wait or very politely say that you're really in a hurry, **Je suis pressé** (Zhuh swee prehssay).

You may hear...

Puis-je vous aider?	*pwee-zhe voos ayday?*	Can I help you?
On s'occupe de vous?	*ohn soccoop duh voo?*	Have you been served?
Quelle taille?	*kel tie?*	What size?
On n'en a pas	*ohn non ah pa*	We don't have any
Voici	*vwassee*	Here you are
Autre chose?	*otruh shoz?*	Anything else?
Je vous l'emballe?	*zhe voo lohmbal?*	Shall I wrap it for you?
C'est...(cinquante) euros	*sey...(sankohnt) uhro*	It's...(50) euros
C'est en solde	*sayt ohn sold*	It's reduced

English newspapers
If you buy your English newspaper in France, be aware that not only will the price be grossly inflated but that it will also have some supplements missing. Make sure you check it's what you want before you buy it.

Where to shop

Where can I find a...	Où puis-je trouver...	oo _pwee_-zhe troo_vay_...
- bookshop?	- une librairie?	- oon lee_bray_ree?
- clothes shop?	- un magasin de vêtements?	- uhn maga_sahn_ duh vet_mohn_?
- department store?	- un centre commercial?	- uhn sohntruh komuhr_syal_?
- gift shop?	- une boutique de cadeaux?	- oon buteek duh kadoh?
- music shop?	- un magasin de musique?	- uhn maga_sahn_ duh moo_zeek_?
- market?	- un marché?	- uhn mar_shay_?
- newsagent?	- un marchand de journaux?	- uhn marshahn duh zhoor_noh_?
- shoe shop?	- un magasin de chaussures?	- uhn maga_sahn_ duh shoh_ssur_?
- stationers?	- une papeterie?	- oon pahpehteree?
- tobacconist?	- un tabac?	- uhn ta_bah_?
- souvenir shop	- un magasin de souvenirs?	- uhn maga_sahn_ duh soov_neer_?
What's the best place to buy...?	Où se trouve le meilleur endroit pour acheter...?	oo suh troove luh _mayur_ _ohn_drewa poor ashuh_tay_...?
I'd like to buy...	J'aimerais acheter...	_jem_maray ashuh_tay_...

35

- a film	**- un film**	*- uhn feelm*
- an English newspaper	**- un journal anglais**	*- un zhoornal ohnglay*
- a map	**- une carte géographique**	*- oon cart jayo-grafeek*
- postcards	**- des cartes postales**	*- dey cart posstall*
- a present	**- un cadeau**	*- uhn kadoh*
- stamps	**- des timbres**	*- dey tambruh*
- sun cream	**- de la crème solaire**	*- duh la krem solair*

Food & markets

Is there a supermarket / market nearby?	**Y a t-il un supermarché/ marché près d'ici?**	*eee ya teel uhn soopairmarshay/ marshay pray d'eecee?*
Can I have ...	**Pourrais-je avoir...**	*pooray-zhe avwar...*
- some bread?	**- du pain?**	*- doo pahn?*
- some fruit?	**- des fruits?**	*- dey frewee?*
- some cheese?	**- du fromage?**	*- doo frohmahzhe?*
- a bottle of water?	**- une bouteille d'eau?**	*- oon bootayuh d'oh?*
- a bottle of wine?	**- une bouteille de vin?**	*- oon bootayuh duh vahn?*
I'd like... of that	**J'aimerais... de ça**	*jemmaray... duh sa*
- half a kilo	**- 500 gr (cinq cent grammes)**	*- sihnk sahn gramm*
- 250 grams	**- deux-cent cinquante grammes**	*- duh-sohn sankohnt gram*
- a small/big piece	**- un petit/gros morceau**	*- uhn puhtee/grow moreso*

Fruit and vegetables

Most supermarkets in France expect you to weigh your fruit and vegetables yourself. Look out for the scales and don't leave without that all-important little sticker, otherwise there'll be drama at the till.

Getting around

Hop between towns on the world-class
rail system. The country suffers from
transport strikes, but overall the trains
are quite reliable and affordable. The
crème de la crème is the TGV, a high-
speed service. However, flights remain a
cheaper and quicker choice for cross-
country jaunts.

The most atmospheric option is driving.
France contains many epic panoramas
and gastronomic finds. The landscape
rewards visitors who take time to
explore it properly.

Arrival

Paris's Charles de Gaulle International Airport, also known as Roissy, is France's main hub and Europe's second busiest, after London Heathrow. Other main entry points include Paris-Orly, Nice Côte d'Azur and Toulouse-Blagnac. Strikes sometimes disrupt service, but otherwise it's business as usual here. However, savvy travellers should double-check ground transport schedules, as some stop rather early in the evening.

Where is/are the...	**Où est/sont ...**	*oo ey/sohn...*
- luggage from flight...?	**- les bagages du vol...?**	*- ley bagazh doo vol...?*
- luggage trolleys?	**- les chariots à bagages?**	*- ley shareeoh ah bagazh?*
- lost luggage office?	**- le bureau des bagages trouvés?**	*- luh booro dey bagazh troovey?*

Where is/are the...	**Où est/sont...**	*oo ey/sohn...*
- buses?	**- les bus?**	*- ley booce?*
- trains?	**- les trains?**	*- ley trahn?*
- taxis?	**- les taxis?**	*- ley taxi?*
- car rental?	**- le bureau de location de voitures?**	*- luh booro de lokasion duh vwa-toor?*
- exit?	**- la sortie?**	*- la sortee?*
How do I get to hotel...?	**Comment fais-je pour aller à l'hôtel...?**	*commuhn fey-zhe pour alley ah loh-tel...?*

My baggage is...	**Mes bagages ont été...**	*mey bagazh ohn etay...*
- lost	**- perdus**	*- pairdo*
- damaged	**- endommagés**	*- ondomazhey*
- stolen	**- voles**	*- volley*

Customs

No comedy at customs: officials tend towards the serious side here. Inspectors usually wave through EU visitors with nothing to declare, though an occasional check may slow the exit stampede. Queuing is still somewhat of a mystery to the French, though the situation's improving.

The children are on this passport	**Les enfants sont sur ce passeport**	_leyz onfohn sohn sooer suh paspore_
We're here on holiday	**Nous sommes ici en vacances**	_noo soms eecee ohn vaconse_
I'm going to ...	**Je vais à...**	_zhuh veyz ah..._
I have nothing to declare	**Je n'ai rien à déclarer**	_zhuh nay ryen a deklarey_
Do I have to declare this?	**Dois-je déclarer ceci?**	_dwa-zhuh deklarey suhsee?_

Car hire

France has the usual choice of big-name brands, available by phone, Internet or in-person booking at airports. Don't trust a local alternative, unless you've received a specific recommendation: horror stories abound.

I'd like to hire a ...	**J'aimerais louer...**	_jemmaray looey..._
- car	**- une voiture**	_- oon vwatoor_
- people carrier with...	**- un monospace avec...**	_- uhn monospass avek ..._
- air conditioning	**- l'air conditionné**	_- lair kondeesyoney_
- automatic transmission	**- transmission automatique**	_- tronzmeessyon automateek_
How much is that for a ...	**C'est combien pour...**	_sey kombyen poor..._
- day?	**- la journée?**	_- la zhoornay?_
- week?	**- la semaine?**	_- la suhmen?_
Does that include...	**Est-ce que ça inclut ...**	_ess kuh sa ankloo ..._
- mileage?	**- le kilométrage?**	_- luh kilomeytrazhe?_
- insurance?	**- l'assurance?**	_- lassooronce?_

Leaded petrol

French stations no longer sell leaded petrol. Some offer lead replacement petrol, known as **Super ARS**, or a lead-substitute, mixed into the tank.

On the road

Cities can be very manic, Marseilles being among the worst offenders. However, traffic nationwide has improved dramatically since the introduction of many, many speed cameras. Drivers have applied the brakes, because French cops are very keen to enforce penalties. Follow their cues.

What is the maximum speed?	**Quel est la vitesse maximale autorisée?**	*kel ey la veetess maxeemal ohtohreezey?*
Can I park here?	**Puis-je me garer ici?**	*pwee-zhuh muh garay eecee?*
Where is a petrol station?	**Où est la station service?**	*oo ey la stasyon sairveess?*
Please fill up the tank with...	**Veuillez remplir le réservoir avec...**	*vuhyay rohnpleer avek...*
- unleaded	**- du sans plomb**	*- doo sohn plom*
- diesel	**- du gazole**	*- doo gazoll*
- lead replacement petrol	**- du super ARS**	*- doo soopair ah airess*
- LPG	**- du GPL**	*- doo jay pey el*

Motorway tolls

French motorways are well organised and have lots of attractive pullouts called **aires**. Here's the drawback: costly **péages** (tolls). Factor these into your travel budget (an online route-planner may prove helpful). The good news is that you can pay by card; much quicker than fumbling for change.

Directions

| Is this the road to...? | **Est-ce que c'est la bonne route pour...?** | *ess kuh sey la bohn root poor...?* |

How do I get to...?	**Je prends quelle direction pour...?**	*zhe prohn kel deereksiohn poor...?*
How far is it to...?	**À quelle distance est...?**	*ah kel deestohnse ey...?*
How long will it take to...?	**Cela prendra combien de temps pour aller à...?**	*suhla prohndra kombyen duh tohn pour alley ah...?*
Could you point it out on the map?	**Pouvez-vous me montrer sur la carte?**	*poovey-voo muh mohntray sooer la kart?*
I've lost my way	**Je me suis perdu**	*zhuh meh swee pairdo*
On the right/left	**Sur la droite/ gauche**	*sooer la dre-wutt/ goshuh*
Turn right/left	**Tournez à droite/ gauche**	*toornay ah dre-wutt/ goshuh*
Straight ahead	**Tout droit**	*too dre-wa*
Turn around	**Faites demi-tour**	*feht duhmee toor*

Buying train tickets

Ask about discounts: the price system teems with special rates for students, families, elderly travellers and more. Be ready to provide proof of status.

Public transport

Bus travel is, frankly, not the preferred option. Rely on these routes only for short hops or to reach rural areas. Otherwise, plump for the train or, in cities like Paris, the superb Métro.

Bus	**Le bus**	*luh booce*
Bus station	**La gare (routière)**	*la gar (rootyair)*
Train	**Le train**	*luh trahn*
Train station	**La gare (ferroviaire)**	*la gar (ferrovyair)*

41

I would like to go to...	J'aimerais aller à...	*jemmaray allay ah...*
I would like a ticket...	J'aimerais un billet...	*jemmaray uhn beeyay...*
- single	- simple	*- sampluh*
- return	- aller-retour	*- allay-ruhtoor*
- first class	- en première classe	*- ahn pruhmyair klass*
- smoking/non-smoking	- fumeur/non-fumeur	*- foomuhr/nohn-foomuhr*
What time does it leave/arrive?	A quelle heure le train part-il?/arrive-t-il?	*ah kel err luh trahn par teel?/areeve-teel?*
Could you tell me when to get off?	Pourriez-vous me dire où descendre?	*pooreeyay-voo muh deer oo dessohn-druh?*

Taxis

I'd like a taxi to...	Je voudrais un taxi pour...	*zhuh voodray uhn taxi poor...*
How much is it to...	C'est combien pour aller...	*sey kombyen pou allay...*
- the airport?	- à l'aéroport?	*- al lairopore?*
- the town centre?	- au centre-ville?	*- oh sohntruh-veel?*
- the hotel?	- à l'hôtel?	*- ah lohtel?*

Tours

Wine tasting is the classic French excursion. Decorum calls for savouring and spitting, but what vacationer stands on ceremony? Motorists should watch for tiny road signs, which often indicate stunning, off-the-beaten-track curiosities.

Are there any organised tours of the town/region?	Y a-t-il des visites guidées de la ville/région?	*ee ya teel day veezeet gheeday duh la veel/rayjyon*
Where do they leave from?	D'où partent-ils?	*doo pahrt-teel?*
What time does it start?	A quelle heure commencent-ils?	*ah kel err komohnce-teel?*
Do you have English-speaking guides?	Avez-vous des guides qui parlent l'anglais?	*avay-voo dey gheed kee parl lohnglay?*

Accommodation

As one of the world's top tourist destinations, France has no shortage of accommodation to offer. While conveniently placed hotels such as those in city centres or next to train stations should be booked in advance, there is a huge number of alternatives available. The star ratings system is stringently applied across the board, as much for camping sites as for city-centre hotels. From a two-star rating onwards, you can expect a good level of comfort. The only real difficulty here is choosing a place to stay among the many on offer.

Purchasing a local guide book and scouring the Internet are the best ways to find your perfect hotel.

Types of accommodation

Hotels in France are more affordable than those in the UK and you can find some real gems in the form of private old houses that have opened up to receive guests. These guest houses can come in any form, from tiny rustic farmhouses to **châteaux**. Find them by consulting a guide on the area, keeping a look-out for signs by the road or asking locals. This, along with a sprinkling of luck, can lead to some very interesting finds indeed. The big cities feature some charming and inexpensive hotels; an online hunt can unearth these little treasures.

I'd like to stay in...	**J'aimerais...**	_jemmaray..._
- an apartment	**- un appartement**	_- uhn appartermuhn_
- a campsite	**- un camping**	_- uhn kohmpeeng_
- a hotel	**- un hôtel**	_- uhn ohtel_
- an apart-hotel	**- une résidence-hôtel**	_- oon rayzeedohnce-ohtel_
- a youth hostel	**- une auberge de jeunesse**	_- oon ohbairzh duh zhuhness_
- a guest house	**- une chambre d'hôtes**	_- oon shombruh dote_

Is it...	**Est-ce que c'est ...**	_ess kuh say..._
- full board?	**- en pension complete?**	_- ahn ponsyon komplett?_
- half board?	**- en demi-pension?**	_- ahn duhmee-ponsyon?_
- self-catering?	**- avec cuisine?**	_- avek kweezeen?_

Reservations

Do you have any rooms available?	**Avez-vous des chambres de libres?**	_avay-voo day shombr duh leebr?_
Can you recommend anywhere else?	**Pouvez-vous me recommander un autre endroit?**	_poovay-voo muh ruhkomonday uhn otrh ohndrewa?_
I'd like to make a reservation for...	**J'aimerais faire une réservation pour...**	_jemmaray fair oon raysairvasyohn poor..._
- tonight	**- ce soir**	_- suh swar_
- one night	**- une nuit**	_- oon nwee_
- two nights	**- deux nuits**	_- duh nwee_
- a week	**- une semaine**	_- oon suhmen_

From...(May 1st) to...(May 8th)	**A partir du ... (premier mai) jusqu'au...(huit mai)**	*ah parteer doo... (pruhmyay may) zhooskoh...(wee may)*

Room types

Single rooms will contain a single bed, suitable for one person only. Doubles are for two, sharing a bed. Twins contain two single beds, and are popular with travelling friends and for children. TVs are a standard feature in hotel rooms, though not to be automatically expected in a guest house. Room size will depend on where you're staying but will tend towards the small. France is a good place to try camping: their star-ratings system is government-regulated and therefore reliable.

Bargain stays

France has cheap, motel-like chains such as those you find in the US. These are found on the motorway and you check-in and pay electronically, using a card. Though basic, they are unfailingly cheap and clean.

Do you have a room...	**Auriez-vous une chambre...**	*ohreeyay-voo oon shombruh...*
- a single	**- simple**	*- sampl*
- a double	**- double**	*- doobl*
- a family with...	**- pour une famille avec...**	*- poor oon fameey avek...*
- a cot?	**- un lit pour enfant?**	*- uhn lee poor ohn-fohn?*
- twin beds?	**- deux lits simples?**	*- duh lee sampl?*
- a double bed?	**- un lit double?**	*- uhn lee doobl?*
- a bath/shower?	**- une salle de bain/ une douche?**	*- oon sal duh bahn/oon doosh?*
- air conditioning?	**- l'air conditionné?**	*- l'air kondeesionay?*
- internet access?	**- accès internet?**	*- axay ahntairnet?*
Can I see the room?	**Puis-je voir la chambre?**	*pwee-zhuh vwar la shombr?*

45

Prices

Breakfast isn't as important to the French as it is to the Brits. Often consisting of just a few pastries and coffee, it's generally not worth paying extra for. As with British hotels, making phone calls from your room will be heavily over-priced as will the mini-bar and services such as dry-cleaning. It isn't necessary to tip the concierge or the maid, but if you use the porter, a €5 tip is the norm. A small tourism tax is sometimes added to your bill. The amount can vary, but the highest rate will be around €1 for each day of your stay.

How much is...	Combien coûte...	kombyen koot...
- a double room?	- une chambre double?	- oon shombruh doobluh?
- per night?	- par nuit?	- par nwee?
- per week?	- par semaine?	- par suhmen?
Is breakfast included?	Le petit-déjeuner est-il compris?	luh puhtee-dayjuhnay ayt-eel kompree?
Do you have a reduction for children?	Faîtes-vous une réduction pour les enfants?	fett-voo oon ray-dooksyon poor leyz ohnfohn?
Do you have a single room supplement?	Y a-t-il un supplément pour une chambre individuelle?	ee yah teel uhn suplayhmahn poor oon shombruh uhndeeveeduhayl
Is there ...	Y a-t-il...	ee ya teel...
- a swimming pool?	- une piscine?	- oon peeseen?
- an elevator?	- un ascenseur?	- uhn assohnsurh?

Hôtel Ritz in Paris

Home to fashion designer Coco Chanel for over 30 years, the Hôtel Ritz was the setting for her scandalous affair with a Nazi officer during World War II.

Home Cooking

In guest houses it's not unusual for the host to provide
dinner for a reasonable fee. This is a great opportunity
to sample authentic French home cooking.

I'll take it	**Je la prends**	*zhuh lah prohn*
Can I pay...	**Puis-je payer...**	*pwee-zhuh payay...*
- by credit card?	**- par carte?**	*- par kart?*
- by traveller's cheque?	**- en traveller's cheque?**	*- ahn travuhlurs check?*

Special requests

Could you...	**Pourriez-vous...**	*pooreeyay-voo...*
- put this in the hotel safe?	**- mettre ceci dans le coffre de l'hôtel?**	*- mettruh suhsee dohn luh koffre duh lohtel?*
- order a taxi for me?	**- me commander un taxi?**	*- muh komohnday uhn taxee?*
- wake me up at 7am?	**- me réveiller à sept heures du matin?**	*- muh rayvayay ah set err doo matahn?*

Can I have...	**Puis-je avoir...**	*pwee-zhuh avwar...*
- a room with a sea view?	**- une chambre avec vue sur la mer?**	*- oon shombruh avek voo sooer la mair?*
- a bigger room?	**- une chambre plus grande?**	*- oon shombruh ploo grohnduh?*
- a quieter room?	**- une chambre plus tranquille?**	*- oon shombruh ploo tronkeel?*

Is there...	**Y a-t-il...**	*ee ya teel...*
- a safe?	**- un coffre?**	*- uhn koffre?*
- a babysitting service?	**- un service de babysitting?**	*- uhn sairveess duh behbee-seeting?*

| - a laundry service? | - un service de nettoyage? | - uhn sair_veess_ duh netwa_yazh_? |
| Is there wheelchair access? | Y a-t-il un accès handicapés? | ee ya teel uhn a_xay_ ohndeeka_pay_? |

Checking in & out

I have a reservation for tonight	J'ai une réservation pour ce soir	zhay oon raysairvasy-_ohn_ poor suh swar
In the name of...	Au nom de...	oh nohm duh...
Here's my passport	Voici mon passeport	vwa_see_ mohn pass-_pore_
What time is check out?	A quelle heure doit-on quitter la chambre?	ah kel err dwa tohn kee_tay_ la shom-bruh?
Can I have a later check out?	Puis-je partir plus tard?	_pwee_-zhuh par_teer_ ploo tar?
Can I leave my bags here?	Puis-je laisser mes bagages ici?	pwee-zhuh leh_ssay_ may ba_gazh_ ee_cee_?
I'd like to check out	J'aimerais quitter l'hôtel	_jem_maray kee_tay_ lohtel
Can I have the bill?	Puis-je avoir la note?	_pwee_-zhuh a_vwar_ la noht?

Camping

Do you have ...	Avez-vous...	a_vay_-voo...
- a site available?	- un emplacement de libre?	- uhn ohmplass_mohn_ duh leebruh?
- electricity?	- l'électricité?	- leh_lektreeseetay_?
- hot showers?	- des douches chaudes?	- dey doosh shohd?
- tents for hire?	- des tentes à louer?	- dey tohnt ah loo_ay_?
How much is it per ...	Quel est le prix par...	kel ay luh pree par...
- tent?	- tente?	- tohnt?
- caravan?	- caravane?	- cara_vahn_?
- person?	- personne?	- pair_sonn_?
- car?	- voiture?	- vwa_toor_?
Where is the...	Où est...	oo ay...
- reception?	- la reception?	- la raysep_syon_?

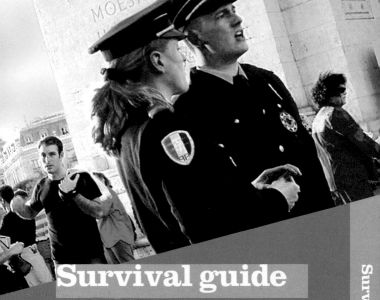

Survival guide

France is often accused of not being in a hurry about anything and it can often seem that way. Whole streets can be closed for lunchtime and trying to find basic services on a Sunday can be an ordeal. Find out in advance what your options are by visiting the Tourist Information Office (**Office de Tourisme**) or by asking the locals. If you're staying in a small town then remember the baker – not only does he know everyone and everything but he'll also be open at lunchtime and on Sundays (and often sell a few extra things such as ground coffee, sandwiches, cola…).

Money & banks

Where is the nearest...	Où est...le/la plus proche?	oo ay...luh/la ploo prosh?
- bank?	- la banque	- la bohnk
- ATM/bank machine?	- le distributeur de billets	- luh deestree-boot*uhr* duh bee*yay*
- foreign exchange office?	- bureau de change	- boo*ro* duh shohnzh
I'd like to...	J'aimerais...	*jem*maray ...
- withdraw money	- retirer de l'argent	- ruhtee*ray* duh lar*zhon*
- cash a traveller's cheque	- encaisser un traveller's cheque	- ohnkay*ssay* uhn travuh*lurs* check
- change money	- changer de l'argent	- shohn*zhay* duh lar*zhon*
- arrange a transfer	- faire un transfert	- fayr uhn trohns*fair*

Banks

As in Britain, banks close early. However, it being France, they also close for two hours at lunchtime, sometimes more. Make sure you find out your bank's opening hours.

What's the exchange rate?	Quel est le taux de change?	kel ay luh toh duh *shohnzh*?
What's the commission?	A combien s'élève la commission?	ah kom*byen* say*lev* la komee*ssyohn*?
What's the charge for...	Quel est le prix pour...	kel ay luh pree poor...

- making a withdrawal	- faire un retrait?	- fair uhn ruhtray?
- exchanging money	- changer de l'argent	- ayshohnjay duh l'arzhon
- cashing a cheque	- encaisser un chèque	- ohnkayssay uhn shek

This is not right	Ce n'est pas exact	suh ney pah exact
Is there a problem with my account?	Y a-t-il un problème sur mon compte?	ee ya teel uhn proh-blehm sooer mohn kohnt?
The ATM/bank machine took my card	Le distributeur a pris ma carte	luh deestreebootuhr ah pree mah kart
I've forgotten my PIN	J'ai oublié mon code	zhay oobleeyay mohn kod

Post office

| Where is the (main) post office? | Où se trouve le (principal) bureau de poste? | oo suh troove luh (prahnceepahl) booro duh pohst? |

I'd like to send a...	J'aimerais envoyer...	jemmaray ohn-vwayay...
- letter	- une lettre	- oon letruh
- postcard	- une carte postale	- oon kart pohstahl
- parcel	- un colis	- uhn kohlee
- fax	- un fax	- uhn fax

I'd like to send this ...	J'aimerais l'envoyer...	jemmaray lohn-vwayay...
- to the United Kingdom	- au Royaume-Uni	- oh rahyohm oonee
- by airmail	- par avion	- par avyon
- by express mail	- en distribution express	- ohn deestreebu-sion express
- by registered mail	- en courrier recommandé	- ohn kooreeyay ruhkohmohndey

I'd like...	J'aimerais...	jemmaray...
- a stamp for this letter/postcard	- un timbre pour cette lettre/carte postale	- uhn tahmbruh poor set lettruh/kart pohstahl
- to buy envelopes	- acheter des enveloppes	- ashuhtay deys ohn-vuhlop

| It contains... | Ça contient... | sa kontyen... |
| It's fragile | C'est fragile | say frajeel |

Generally speaking
Even if the staff speak English, making the effort to use some French will considerably improve the service you receive.

Telecoms

Where can I make an international phone call?	Où puis-je téléphoner à l'étranger?	oo pwee-zhuh teyley-fohnay ah letrohn-jay?
Where can I buy a phone card?	Où puis-je acheter une carte téléphonique?	oo pwee-zhuh ashuh-tay oon kart teyley-fohneek?
How do I call abroad?	Comment fais-je pour téléphoner à l'étranger?	kohmohn fey-zhuh poor teyleyfohnay ah letrohnjay?
How much does it cost per minute?	Combien coûte la minute?	kombyen koot la meenoot?
The number is...	Le numéro est...	luh noomayro ay...
What's the area/country code for...?	Quelle est l'indicatif régional/pays pour...?	kel ay lahndeekateef rayzhiohnal/payee poor...?
The number is engaged	Le numéro est occupé	luh noomayro ayt ohkoopay
The connection is bad	La connection est mauvaise	la konexiohn ay moh-vayse
I've been cut off	J'ai été coupé	zhay ehtay koopay

I'd like...	J'aimerais...	_jemmaray..._
- a charger for my mobile phone	- un chargeur pour mon téléphone mobile	- _uhn sharjur poor mohn teyleyfohn mohbeel_
- an adaptor plug	- une multiprise	- _oon multeepreeze_

Internet

Where's the nearest Internet café?	Où est le café internet le plus proche?	_oo ay luh kafay ahn-tairnet luh ploo prosh?_
Can I access the Internet here?	Puis-je avoir accès à internet ici?	_pwee-zhuh avwar axay ah ahntairnet eecee?_

I'd like to...	J'aimerais...	_jemmaray..._
- use the Internet	- utiliser internet	- _ooteeleesay ahntairnet_
- check my email	- lire mes e-mails	- _leer mez ee-mell_
- use a printer	- me servir d'une imprimante	- _muh sairveer doon ahmpreemohnte_

How much is it...	Combien coûte...	_kombyen koot..._
- per minute?	- la minute?	- _la meenoot?_
- per hour?	- l'heure?	- _lerr?_
- to buy a CD?	- un CD?	- _uhn sehdeh?_

How do I...	Comment est-ce que...	_komohn ess kuh..._
- log on?	- je me connecte?	- _zhe meh konekt?_
- open a browser?	- j'ouvre un navigateur	- _j'oovruh uhn navee-gatuhr?_
- print this?	- j'imprime ceci?	- _jampreem suhsee?_

I need help with this computer	J'ai besoin d'aide avec cet ordinateur	_zhay buhswan ded avek set ordeenah-tuhr_
The computer has crashed	Cet ordinateur est tombé en panne	_set ordeenatuhr ay tombay ohn pan_
I've finished	J'ai fini	_zhay feenee_

Chemist

Where's the nearest (all-night) pharmacy?	**Où se trouve la pharmacie (de garde) la plus proche?**	*oo suh troov la farmacee (duh gard) la plu prohsh?*
What time does the pharmacy open/close?	**Quelles sont les heures d'ouverture de la pharmacie?**	*kel sohn ley err doovairtoor duh la farmacee?*
I need something for...	**J'ai besoin de quelque chose pour...**	*zhay buhswan duh kelkuhshows poor...*
- diarrhoea	**- la diarrhée**	*- la dyarray*
- a cold	**- le rhume**	*- luh rum*
- a cough	**- la toux**	*- la too*
- insect bites	**- les piqûres d'insectes**	*- lay peekoor dahnsect*
- sunburn	**- un coup de soleil**	*- uhn koo duh solayy*
- hay fever	**- le rhume des foins**	*- luh rum dey fwahn*
- period pain	**- les règles douloureuses**	*- ley regluh doolooreuz*
- abdominal pains	**- des douleurs abdominales**	*- dey dooluhr abdohmeenal*
- a urine infection	**- une infection urinaire**	*- oon ahnfexion ooreenair*
I'd like...	**J'aimerais...**	*jemmaray...*
- aspirin	**- de l'aspirine**	*- duh laspeereen*
- condoms	**- des préservatifs**	*- dey preysairvateef*
- insect repellent	**- un spray pour les insects**	*- uhn spray poor leyz inhsekt*
- painkillers	**- des analgésiques**	*- dey anahlzhayzeek*
- a contraceptive	**- un contraceptif**	*- uhn contrasepteef*
How much should I take?	**Combien devrais-je en prendre?**	*kombyen duhvray-zhuh ahn prohndruh?*
Take...	**Prenez...**	*pruhnay...*
- a tablet (every... hours)	**- un cachet (toutes les...heures)**	*- uhn kashay (toot lay ...err)*
- a teaspoon	**- une cuillère à café**	*- oon kweeyair ah kafay*

- with water	- avec de l'eau	_avek duh loh_
How often should I take this?	Quand devrais-je le prendre?	_kohn duhvray-zhuh luh prohndruh?_
- once/twice a day	- une/deux fois par jour	_- oon/duh fwa par zhoor_
- before/after meals	- avant/après les repas	_- ahvohn/apray lay ruhpar_
- in the morning/evening	- le matin/soir	_- luh matahn/swar_
Is it suitable for children?	Est-ce que ça convient à un enfant?	_ess kuh sa konvyen ah uhn ohnfohn?_
Will it make me drowsy?	Est-ce que ça peut provoquer des fatigues?	_ess kuh sa peh provohkay dey fateeg?_
Do I need a prescription?	Me faut-il une ordonnance?	_- muh foht-eel oon ordonohnce?_

Children

Where should I take the children?	Où devrais-je envoyer les enfants?	_oo duhvray-zhuh ohnvwayay leyz ohnfohn?_
Where is the nearest...	Où se trouve... le/la plus près?	_oo suh troov... luh/la ploo pray?_
- playground?	- le jardin d'enfants	_- luh zhardahn dohnfohn_
- fairground?	- la fête foraine	_- la fet fohrain_
- zoo?	- le zoo	_- luh zo-oh_
- swimming pool?	- la piscine	_- la peeseen_
- park?	- le parc	_- luh park_
Is this suitable for children?	Est-ce que ça convient pour les enfants?	_ess kuh sa konvyen poor leyz ohnfohn?_
Are children allowed?	Peut-on amener des enfants?	_pehtohn amehney deyz ohnfohn?_
Are there baby-changing facilities here?	Y a-t-il une table à langer?	_ee ya teel oon tabluh ah lohnzhay?_
Do you have...	Avez-vous...	_avay-voo..._

- a children's menu?	- un menu enfant?	- uhn muhnoo ohnfohn?
- a high chair?	- une chaise haute?	- oon shayz oht?
Is there...	Y a-t-il...	ee ya teel...
- a child-minding service?	- une garde d'enfants?	- oon gard dohnfohn?
- a nursery?	- une garderie?	- oon garduhree?

Children's activities

Beaches sometimes run playgroups for children. The French are obsessed with education and these games and activities will often involve learning something new.

Can you recommend a reliable babysitter?	Pouvez-vous me recommander une baby-sitter fiable?	poovay-voo muh ruhkohmonday oon behbee-seetuhr fyabluh?
He/she is...years old	Il/elle a...ans	eel/ell ah...ohn
I'd like to buy ...	J'aimerais acheter...	jemmaray ashuhtay...
- nappies	- des couches	- dey koosh
- baby wipes	- des lingettes	- dey lahnjet
- tissues	- des kleenex	- dey kleenex

Travellers with disabilities

| I have a disability | Je suis handicapé | zhuh swee ohndeekapay |

I need assistance	**J'ai besoin d'assistance**	*zhay buhswan dasseesstohnce*
I am blind	**Je suis aveugle**	*zhuh swees avuhgluh*
I am deaf	**Je suis sourd**	*zhuh swee soor*
I have a hearing aid	**J'ai une aide auditive**	*zhay oon ed ohdee-teev*
I can't walk well	**Je n'arrive pas bien à marcher**	*zhuh nareev pa byen ah marshay*
Is there a lift?	**Y a-t-il un ascenseur?**	*ee ya teel uhn assohnssurh?*
Is there wheelchair access?	**Y a-t-il un accès handicapés?**	*ee ya teel uhn axay ohndeekapay?*
Can I bring my guide dog?	**Puis-je apporter mon chien d'aveugle?**	*pwee-zhuh aportay mohn shyahn davuhrgluh?*
Are there disabled toilets?	**Y a t-il des toilettes pour handicapés?**	*ee ya teel dey twalett poor ohndeekapay?*
Do you offer disabled services?	**Offrez-vous des services pour handicapés?**	*offray-voo dey sairveess poor ohn-deekapay?*
Could you help me...	**Pourriez-vous m'aider...**	*pooreeyay-voo may-day...*
- cross the street?	**- à traverser la route?**	*- ah trahvairsay la root?*
- go up/down the stairs?	**- à monter/ descendre les marches?**	*- ah montay/ daysohndruh ley marsh?*

Repairs & cleaning

This is broken	**C'est cassé**	*say kassay*
Can you fix it?	**Pouvez-vous le réparer?**	*poovay-voo luh rayparay?*
Do you have...	**Avez-vous...**	*avay-voo...*
- a battery?	**- une pile?**	*- oon peel?*
- spare parts?	**- une pièce de rechange?**	*- oon peeyayss duh ruhshohnge?*
Can you...this?	**Pouvez-vous... ceci?**	*poovay-voo... suhsee?*
- clean	**- nettoyer**	*- netwayay*
- press	**- repasser**	*- ruhpassay*

- dry-clean	- nettoyer à sec	- netwayay ah sek
- patch	- rapiécer	- rapyaysay
When will it be ready?	Quand est-ce que ce sera prêt?	kohn ess kuh suh suhra prey?

Tourist information

Where's the Tourist Information Office?	Où se trouve l'Office de Tourisme?	oo suh troov loffeess duh toureesm?
Do you have a city/regional map?	Avez-vous une carte de la ville/région?	avay-voo oon kart duh lah veel/rayzhyon?
What are the main places of interest?	Quels sont les principales centres d'intérêt?	kel sohn lay prahnseepahl sohntruh dahntayray?
Could you show me on the map?	Pourriez-vous me montrer sur la carte?	pooreeyay-voo muh mohntray sur la kart?
Do you have a brochure in English?	Avez-vous une brochure en anglais?	avay-voo oon brohshoor ohn ohnglay?
We're interested in...	...nous intéresse	...nooz antayress
- history	- l'histoire	- leestwahr
- architecture	- l'architecture	- larsheetektur
- shopping	- le shopping	- luh shohpeeng
- hiking	- la randonnée	- lah rohndonnay
- a scenic walk	- une ballade scénique	- oon balahd sayneek
- a boat cruise	- une croisière en bateau	- oon krewazyair ohn batoh
- a guided tour	- une visite guidée	- oon veezeet guiday
What days is it open/closed?	Quels sont les jours d'ouverture?	kel sohn ley zherr doovairtur?
What time does it open/close?	Quels sont leyz heures d'ouverture?	kel sohn leyz err doovairtoor?
What's the admission price?	Combien coûte une entrée?	kohmbiehn koot dohntray?
Are there any tours in English?	Y a t-il des visites guidées en anglais?	ee ya teel dey veezeet guiday ohn ohnglay?

Emergencies

In case of medical emergency, head to any hospital emergency room whether private or public, regardless of your health insurance status. Both are legally required to assist you, as long as they agree that it is indeed an emergency situation. If you cannot get to a hospital, call the "**pompiers**" (fire brigade and rescue service) by dialling the number 18. Chemists ("**pharmacies**") are easy to find: just look for the green neon cross and a serpent sign.

Medical

Where is...	Où est...	oo ay...
- the hospital?	- l'hôpital?	- lopeetahl?
- the health centre?	- le centre médical?	- luh sohntruh mehdeekal?

I need...	Il me faut...	eel muh foh...
- a doctor	- un docteur	- uhn doctuhr
- a female doctor	- une femme docteur	- oon fam doctuhr
- an ambulance	- une ambulance	- oon ambulance
It's very urgent	C'est très urgent	sey treyz oorjahn
I'm injured	Je suis blessé	zhuh swee blessay

Can I see the doctor?	Puis-je voir le docteur?	pwee-zhuh vwar luh doctuhr?
I don't feel well	Je ne me sens pas bien	zhuh nuh muh sohn pah byen

I have...	J'ai...	zhay...
- a cold	- un rhume	- uhn rûm
- diarrhoea	- la diarrhée	- la dyarray
- a rash	- une rougeur	- oon roozhur
- a temperature	- une forte température	- oon fort tahn-payratur
I have a lump here	J'ai une grosseur ici	zhay oon grossuhr eecee
Can I have the morning-after pill?	Je voudrais la pilule du lendemain	zhuh voodray la peelul doo landuhmuhn
It hurts here	Ça fait mal ici	sa fey mal eecee
It hurts a lot / a little	Ça fait très mal / un peu mal	sa fey trey mal/uhn puh mal

How much do I owe you?	Combien je vous dois?	kombyen zhuh voo dwa?
I have insurance	Je suis assuré/e	zhuh swee assurray

Dentist

I need a dentist	Il me faut un dentiste	eel muh foh uhn danteest
I have tooth ache	J'ai mal aux dents	zhay mal oh dahn
My gums are swollen	Mes gencives sont enflées	mey zhonseeve sohn ohnflay

This filling has fallen out	Ce plombage a sauté	*suh plombazh ah sohtay*
I have an abscess	J'ai un abscès	*zhay uhn absay*
I've broken a tooth	Je me suis cassé une dent	*zhuh muh swee cassay oon dahn*
Are you going to take it out?	Allez-vous l'enlever?	*allay-voo lanluhvay?*
Can you fix it temporarily?	Pouvez-vous faire un soin temporaire?	*poovay-voo fair uhn swohn tohmporair?*

Crime

I want to report a theft	Je veux signaler un vol	*zhuh vuh seenyalay uhn vol*
Someone has stolen my...	On a volé...	*on ah volay...*
- bag	- mon sac	- *mon sak*
- car	- ma voiture	- *mah vwatur*
- credit cards	- mes cartes de crédit	- *mey kart duh creydee*
- money	- mon argent	- *mohn arzhohn*
- passport	- mon passport	- *mohn passpore*
I've been attacked	On m'a attaqué	*on mah atakay*

Lost property

I've lost my...	J'ai perdu...	*zhay pairdu...*
- car keys	- mes clés de voiture	- *may klay duh vwatoor*
- driving licence	- mon permis de conduire	- *mohn pairmee duh kondweer*
- handbag	- mon sac-à-main	- *mohn sak-a-mahn*
- flight tickets	- mes billets d'avion	- *mey beeyay davyon*
It happened...	C'est arrive ...	*sayt areevay ...*
- this morning	- ce matin	- *suh matahn*
- today	- aujourd'hui	- *ohzhoordwee*
- in the hotel	- dans l'hôtel	- *dohn l'ohtel*
I left it in the taxi	Je l'ai laissé dans le taxi	*zhuh lay layssay dohn luh taxee*

Breakdown

| I've had... | J'ai eu... | *zhay ooh...* |
| - an accident | - un accident | - *uhn axeedohn* |

- a breakdown	- une panne	- oon pann
- a puncture	- une crevaison	- oon kruhvay_sohn_
My battery is flat	**Ma batterie est à plat**	mah batter_ee_ ay ah pla
I don't have a spare tyre	**Je n'ai pas de pneu de secours**	zhuh nay pa duh pnuh duh suh_koor_
I've run out of petrol	**Je n'ai plus d'essence**	zhuh nay ploo dayssahnss
My car doesn't start	**Ma voiture refuse de démarrer**	ma vwa_toor_ ruh_fooz_ duh _daymahray_
Can you repair it?	**Pouvez-vous le réparer?**	_poo_vay-voo luh reh-pa_ray_?
How long will you be?	**Ça prendra combien de temps?**	sa prohn_dra_ kom_byen_ duh tohn?
I have breakdown cover	**Je suis couvert pour les pannes d'automobile**	zhuh swee koo_vair_ poor ley pann dohtomoh_beel_

Getting pulled over

The French police can be subtle when signalling you to pull over, so be alert for understated gestures when you see them. They also like to check cars randomly so don't panic if you are stopped.

Problems with the authorities

I'm sorry, I didn't realise...	**Je m'excuse, je n'avais pas réalisé que...**	zhuh mex_kooz_, zhuh navay paj ray-alee_say_ kuh...
- I was driving so fast	**- je conduisais aussi vite**	- zhuh kondwee_zay_ ossee veet
- I went over the red lights	**- j'avais passé un feu rouge**	- zha_vay_ pa_ssay_ uhn fuh roozhe
- it was against the law	**- c'était contraire à la loi**	- seh_tay_ kon_trair_ a la lwa
Here are my documents	**Voici mes papiers**	vwa_see_ may _pa_pyay
I'm innocent	**Je suis innocent**	zhuh sweez eeno_sohn_

Dictionary

This section consists of two parts: an English-French dictionary to help you get your point across and a French-English one to decipher the reply. In the French, we list nouns with their article: **le** for masculine, **la** for feminine and **les** for plural. If nouns can be either masculine or feminine, we display both: **l'ami/e** (friend) means **l'ami** is a male friend, **l'amie** the female version.

For more on grammar, including conjugation of verbs (given here in the "to do" form), and the order of words in sentences, please see the Introduction.

English-French dictionary

A

a(n)	un/une	uhn/oon
about (concerning)	à propos de	ah prohpoh duh
accident	l'accident	l'axeedohn le
accommodation	le logement	lohzhmohn luh
A&E	le service des urgences	sairveess deyz oorzhonce
aeroplane	l'avion	l'avyohn

ago	**il y a**	*eel ee ya*

In French, this expression works differently, instead of saying "(two days) ago", one will say **il y a (deux jours)**

AIDS	le SIDA	luh seeda
airmail	la poste aérienne	lah pohst ah-air-ryen
airport	l'aéroport	l'airopore
alarm	l'alarme	l'alahrm
all	tout	tooh
allergy	l'allergie	l'alairjee
all right	Ok/d'accord	okay/dahkor
ambulance	l'ambulance	l'ohmboolohnce
and	et	eh
any	n'importe (la) quell(le)	namport lakell
America	l'Amérique	l'amayreek
American	américain	amayreekahn
apartment	l'appartement	l'apartuhmohn
April	avril	avreel
area	la région	lah rayzhion
around	autour	otoor
to arrange	arranger	ahrohnjay
arrival	l'arrivée	l'ahreevey
to ask	demander	duhmohndey
aspirin	l'aspirine	l'aspeereen
at	à	ah
August	août	oot
Australia	l'Australie	l'ostralee
Australian	australien	ostraleeyehn

B

back (place)	retour	ruhtoor
baggage	les bagages	lay bagazh
bar (pub)	le bar	luh bahr
to be	être	ehtruh
beach	la plage	lah plazh
because	parce que	parse kuh
best	le meilleur	luh meyur

bill	l'addition	ladisyohn
bit (a)	un peu	uhn puh
boarding card	la carte d'embarquemnt	lah kart d'ohmbarkuh-mohn
book	le livre	luh leevr
to book	réserver	reysairvey
booking	la réservation	lah reysairvasyohn
box office	le guichet / la caisse	luh geeshay / la kayss
boy	le garçon	luh garsohn
brother	le frère	luh frair

bullfight **la corrida** *lah curida*
The style of bullfighting that France is famous for is a principally bloodless sport and involves the bullfighter attempting to snatch a rosette placed on the bull's head.

bureau de change	le bureau de change	luh booro duh shohnzhuh
to burn	brûler	brooley
bus	le bus	luh booce
business	les affaires	layz affair
but	mais	may
to buy	acheter	ashuhtay
by (via)	par	par
by (beside)	près de	prey duh
by (by air, car, etc)	en	ahn

C

café	le café	luh kafay
to call	appeler	appuhlay
camera	l'appareil photo	l'apparay fotoh
can (to be able)	pouvoir	poovwar
to cancel	annuler	anooley
car	la voiture	lah vwatoor
cash	du liquide	doo leekeed
cash point	le distributeur automatique de billets	luh deestreebootur automateek duh beeyay
casino	le casino	luh caseeno
cathedral	la cathédrale	lah kataydrahl
CD	le cd	luh seydey
centre	le centre	luh sohntr
to change	changer	shohnzhay
charge	la charge	lah sharzhuh
to charge	faire payer	fair payay
cheap	pas cher	pah shayr
to check in (airport)	enregistrer ses bagages	ahnrezheestray se bahgazh
to check in (hotel)	se présenter	suh praysohntay
cheque	le chèque	luh shek
child	l'enfant	l'ohnfohn
church	l'église	l'ehgleez

cigarette	**la cigarette**	*lah seegaret*
cinema	**le cinéma**	*luh seenaymah*
city	**la grande ville**	*lah grohnde veel*
close by	**près**	*prey*
to close	**fermer**	*fairmay*
closed	**fermé**	*fairmay*
clothes	**les vêtements**	*lay vetmohn*
club	**la boîte de nuit**	*lah bwat duh nwee*
coast	**la côte**	*lah kot*
cold	**froid**	*frwa*
colour	**la couleur**	*lah koolerr*
to come	**venir**	*vuhneer*
complaint	**la plainte**	*lah plantuh*
to confirm	**confirmer**	*kohnfeermey*
confirmation	**la confirmation**	*lah kohnfeermasion*
consulate	**le consulat**	*luh konsulah*
to contact	**contacter**	*contactey*
contagious	**contagieux**	*kontazhyuh*

cool	**frais**	*frey*

The French also use the slang word **cool** just as the English do, to denote something good or fashionable

cost	**le coût**	*luh koo*
to cost	**coûter**	*kootey*
country	**le pays**	*luh payee*
countryside	**la campagne**	*lah kampanyuh*
cream	**la crème**	*lah krem*
credit card	**la carte de crédit**	*lah kart duh kraydee*
crime	**le crime**	*luh kreem*
currency	**la monnaie**	*lah monnay*
customer	**le client**	*luh cleeyohn*
customs	**la douane**	*lah dawn*
cut	**la coupure**	*lah koopoor*
to cut	**couper**	*coopay*

cycling	**le cyclisme**	*luh seeklismuh*

The French are keen cyclists and it's very easy to find bicycles to rent for the day – a great way to see the sights.

D

to damage	**abîmer**	*abeemay*
danger	**le danger**	*luh dohnzhay*
date (calendar)	**la date**	*lah dat*
daughter	**la fille**	*lah feeyuh*
day	**le jour**	*luh zhoor*
December	**décembre**	*daysohmbruh*
to dehydrate	**se déshydrater**	*suh dayseedratay*
delay	**le retard**	*luh retar*
to dial	**faire un numéro**	*fair uhn noomayro*
difficult	**difficile**	*deefeeseal*

directions	les directions	lay deereksion
dirty	sale	sal
disabled	handicapé	ohndeekapay
discount	la réduction	lah raydooksion
to disturb	déranger	dayrohnjay
doctor	le médecin	luh mehduhsahn
double	double	doobluh
down	en bas	ohn ba
to drive	conduire	kondweer
driver	le conducteur	luh kondukterr
drug	la drogue	lah drog
to dry clean	nettoyer à sec	netwayay ah sek
dry cleaner's	la teinturerie	lah tahntooruhree
during	pendant	pohndohn
duty (tax)	les taxes	lay tax

E

early	tôt	toh
to eat	manger	mohnzhay
e-mail	l'e-mail /la messagerie électronique	luh ee-mell/ la messajuhree elektroneek
embassy	l'ambassade	l'ohmbassad
emergency	l'urgence	l'oorjohnse
England	l'Angleterre	l'ohngluhtair
English	anglais	ohnglay
enough	assez	assay
error	l'erreur	l'ehruhrr
exactly	exactement	exactuhmohn
exchange rate	le taux d'échange	luh toh d'ayshohnje
exhibition	l'exposition	l'exposeesion
to export	exporter	exportay
express (delivery)	la distribution express	lah deestreebusion express
express (train)	le train rapide	luh trahn rapeed

F

facilities	moyen	mwayen
far	loin	lwahn
fast	rapide	rapeed
father	le père	luh pair
to fax	faxer	faxay
favourite	préféré	prayfayray
filling (station)	la station-service	lah stasiohn-sairveess
film (cinema)	le film	luh feelm
film (camera)	la pélicule	lah peyleekul
to finish	finir	feeneer
fire	le feu	luh fuh
fire alarm	l'alarme incendie	l'alahrm ahnsohndee
fire exit	la sortie de secours	lah sortee duh suhkoor
first aid	les premiers secours	lay pruhmyay suhkoor

fitting room	la cabine d'essayage	lah kabeen d'essayazh
flight	le vol	luh vol
flu	la grippe	lah greep
food poisoning	l'intoxication alimentaire	l'ahntoxykasion ahleemohntair
for	pour	poor
February	février	fevreeyay

| **football** | **le football** | *luh footboll* |

No-one in France calls football by its full name, it's always **le foot**. It is a national obsession, but beware of taking young children: the matches can get rough.

form (document)	le formulaire	luh formoolair
free (vacant)	libre	leebruh
free (money)	gratuit	gratwee
friend	l'ami/e	l'amee
from	de	duh
furnished	meublé	muhblay

G
gallery	la galerie	lah galuhree
garage	le garage	luh garazh
gas	le gaz	luh gaz
gents (toilets)	les messieurs (toilettes)	lay maysyuh (twalayt)
to get	obtenir	obtuhneer
girl	la fille	lah feey
to give	donner	donnay
glasses (sight)	des lunettes	dey loonett
to go	aller	allay
golf	le golf	luh golf
golf course	le parcours de golf	luh parkoor duh golf
good	bien	byen
group	le groupe	luh groop
guarantee	la garantie	lah garohntee
guide	le guide	luh geed

H
hair	les cheveux	lay shuhvuh
half	un demi	uhn duhmee
to have	avoir	avwar
heat	la chaleur	lah shaluhr
help!	au secours!	oh suhkoor!
to help	aider	ayday
here	ici	eecee
high	haut	oh
to hire	louer	looay
holiday	le jour férié	feyreeyay
holidays	les vacances	lay vakohnse

homosexual **homosexuel** *ohmoseksuahl*
The French, especially the younger generations, tend to use the English word "gay", which is also a perfectly acceptable term to use.

horse riding	l'équitation	*l'ehkeetasyon*
hospital	l'hôpital	*l'opeetal*
hot	chaud	*show*
how?	comment?	*kommohn?*
how big?	quelle taille?	*kel tie?*
how far?	à quelle distance?	*ah kel deestohnce?*
how long?	quelle longueur?	*kel longuhr?*
how much?	combien?	*kombyen?*
to be hungry	avoir faim	*avwar fahm*
hurry up!	dépêche-toi! (polite: dépêchez-vous!)	*daypesh twa! (daypeshay-voo!)*
to hurt	faire mal	*fair mal*
husband	le mari	*luh mare*

I

identity card	la carte d'identité	*lah kart d'eedenteetay*
ill	malade	*malahd*
important	important	*amportohn*
in	dans	*dohn*
information	l'information	*l'anformasion*
inside	à l'interieur	*ah l'anteyreeyur*
insurance	l'assurance	*l'assoorohnce*
interesting	intéressant	*anteyreyssohn*
international	international	*antairnasional*
Ireland	l'Irlande	*l'earlohnde*
Irish	irlandais	*earlohnday*
island	l'île	*l'eel*
itinerary	l'itinéraire	*l'eeteenayrair*

J

January	janvier	*zhonvyay*
jellyfish	la méduse	*lah maydooze*
jet ski	le jet ski	*luh jet-skee*
journey	le voyage	*luh vwayazh*
June	juin	*jwahn*

July **Juillet** *Jweeyay*
July 14th is Bastille Day, France's national day. You can expect fireworks, speeches and parades as part of the celebrations.

junction	le carrefour	*luh karfoor*
just (only)	seulement	*suluhmohn*

K

to keep	garder	*garday*

English	French	Pronunciation
key	la clé	lah clay
keyboard	le clavier	luh clavyay
key ring	le porte-clé	luh portuh-clay
kid	le gamin	luh gamahn
to kill	tuer	tuh-eh
kind (nice)	sympa	sahmpa
kind (sort)	le genre	luh zhonr
kiosk	le kiosque	luh kiosk
kiss	le baiser	luh bayzay
to kiss	embrasser	ohmbrassay
to knock	frapper	frappay
to know (person)	connaître	conaytruh
to know (knowledge)	savoir	savwar

L

English	French	Pronunciation
label	l'étiquette	l'ehteeket
ladies (toilets)	les dames (toilettes)	lay dam (twalayhtt)
lady	la dame	lah dam
language	le langage	luh lohngazh
last	le dernier	luh dairnyay
late (delayed)	retardé	ruhtarday
late (time)	en retard	ohn ruhtar
launderette	la laverie automatique	lah lavree autohmateek
lawyer	l'avocat	l'ahvoka
to leave	partir	parteer
left	gauche	gohsh
less	moins	mwahn
letter	la lettre	lah lettruh
library	la bibliothèque	lah beebleeyotek
lifeguard	le maître-nageur	luh mehtr-nazhur
life jacket	le gilet de sauvetage	luh zheelay duh sohvuhtazh
lift	l'ascenseur	l'assohnssuhr
to like	aimer	aymay
to listen to	écouter	aykootay
little (a little)	un petit peu	uhn puhtee
local	local/du coin	puh lowkahl/ doou kwan
to look	regarder	ruhgarday
to lose	perdre	pairdruh
lost property	les objets trouvés	layz objay troovay
luggage	les bagages	lay bagazh

M

English	French	Pronunciation
madam	madame	madahm
mail	le courrier	luh kooreeyay
main	principal	pranseepahl
main road	la route principale	lah root pranseepahl
to make	faire	fair
man	l'homme	l'ohm
manager	le gérant	luh zhayrohn
many	beaucoup de	bohkoo
map (city)	la carte	lah kart
map (road)	la carte	lah kart

| March | **mars** | *marce* |
| market | **le marché** | *luh mar<u>shay</u>* |

married **marié** *maree<u>yay</u>*
French church weddings are merely ceremonial, the legal marriage must take place at the town hall. In France, getting married is also known as "going before the mayor".

material (cloth)	**tissu**	*<u>tees</u>soo*
May	**mai**	*mey*
maybe	**peut-être**	*puht-ehtruh*
mechanic	**le mécanicien**	*luh mehkanee<u>syan</u>*
to meet	**rencontrer**	*rohnkontrey*
meeting	**la réunion**	*lah rayu<u>niohn</u>*
message	**le message**	*luh mey<u>ssazh</u>*
midday	**le midi**	*luh mee<u>dee</u>*
midnight	**le minuit**	*luh meen<u>wee</u>*
minimum	**minimum**	*mini<u>murm</u>*
minute	**la minute**	*lah mee<u>nut</u>*
to miss (a person)	**(...) me manque**	*(...) muh mohnk*
to miss (a train)	**manquer**	*mohn<u>kay</u>*
missing	**manquant**	*mohn<u>kohn</u>*
mobile phone	**le téléphone mobile**	*luh teyley<u>fon</u> moh<u>beel</u>*
moment	**le moment**	*luh moh<u>mohn</u>*
money	**l'argent**	*l'ar<u>zhohn</u>*
more	**plus**	*pluce*
mosquito	**la moustique**	*lah moo<u>steek</u>*
most (of)	**la plupart (de)**	*lah plu<u>par</u> (duh)*
mother	**la mère**	*lah mair*
much	**beaucoup de**	*boh<u>koo</u> duh luh*
museum	**le musée**	*moo<u>zay</u>*
musical	**la comédie musicale**	*lah komay<u>dee</u> moozee<u>kahl</u>*
must	**devoir**	*duh<u>vwar</u>*

my **mon/ma/mes** *mohn/mar/may*
If what you're describing belongs to a female person or object, then use ma, if it belongs to a male person or a object, use mon. Use mes when referring to plurals, e.g. mes parents (my parents).

N

name	**le nom**	*luh nohm*
nationality	**la nationalité**	*lah nassyonalee<u>tay</u>*
near	**près de**	*prey duh*
necessary	**nécessaire**	*neysay<u>sair</u>*
to need	**avoir besoin de**	*avwar buh<u>swan</u> duh*
never	**jamais**	*zha<u>may</u>*
new	**nouveau**	*noo<u>voh</u>*
news	**les informations**	*ley ahnformas<u>syohn</u>*
newspaper	**le journal**	*luh zhoor<u>nahl</u>*

next	**prochain**	*prohshahn*
next to	**à côté de**	*ah kohtay duh*
nice (people)	**gentil**	*zhontee*
nice (things)	**sympa**	*sahmpa*
night	**la nuit**	*lah nwee*
nightclub	**la boîte de nuit**	*lah bwat duh nwee*
north	**nord**	*nor*
note (money)	**le billet**	*luh beeyay*
nothing	**rien**	*ryahn*
November	**novembre**	*nohvombruh*
now	**maintenant**	*mahntuhnohn*
nowhere	**nulle part**	*nul par*
nudist beach	**la plage nudiste**	*lah plazh nudeest*

> **number** **le nombre** *luh nohmbruh*
> In the case of a phone number, the word to use
> is numéro.

O

| object | **l'objet** | *l'objay* |

> **October** **octobre** *octohbruh*
> The French have increasingly begun to celebrate
> Halloween in the past few years, so look out for
> special events that may be happening.

off (food)	**périmé**	*payreemay*
off (switched)	**éteint**	*ehtahn*
office	**le bureau**	*luh buro*
OK	**d'accord**	*d'ackor*
on	**sur**	*suhr*
once	**une fois**	*oon fwa*
only	**seulement**	*sulmohn*
open	**ouvert**	*oovair*
to open	**ouvrir**	*oovreer*
operator	**l'opérateur**	*l'opehratuhr*
opposite (place)	**en face de**	*ohn fars duh*
optician's	**l'opticien**	*l'opteesyen*
or	**ou**	*oo*
to order	**commander**	*komohnday*
other	**autre**	*ohtr*
outdoor	**à l'extérieur**	*ah l'exteyreeyur*
out of order	**hors service**	*ohr sairveess*
outside	**dehors**	*duh-or*
overnight	**du jour au lendemain**	*doo zhoor oh lohnduhmahn*
owner	**le propriétaire**	*luh propreeyaytair*
oxygen	**l'oxygène**	*l'oxeejain*

P

| painkiller | **l'analgésique** | *l'ahnaljayzeek* |

pair	**la paire**	*lah pair*
parents	**les parents**	*lay parohn*
park	**le parc**	*luh park*
to park	**se garer**	*suh garay*
passport	**le passeport**	*luh passpore*
to pay	**payer**	*payay*
people	**les gens**	*lay zhon*
perhaps	**peut-être**	*puht-ehtruh*
person	**la personne**	*lah pairsohn*
phone	**le téléphone**	*luh teyleyfohn*
to phone	**téléphoner**	*teyleyfohnay*
photo	**la photo**	*lah fotoh*
phrase book	**le recueil d'expressions**	*luh ruhkuhyuh d'expressyon*
place	**l'endroit**	*l'ohndrewa*
platform (train)	**le quai**	*luh kay*
police	**la police**	*lah poleece*
port (drink)	**le porto**	*luh poretoh*

| port (sea) | **le port** | *luh pore* |

Marseilles is one of France's most important ports and because of this boasts a diverse ethnicity and lively African feel.

possible	**possible**	*posseebluh*
post	**le courrier**	*luh kooreeyay*
post office	**le bureau de poste**	*luh buro duh pohst*
to prefer	**préférer**	*preyfeyray*
prescription	**la prescription**	*lah prescreepsion*
pretty	**joli**	*zhohlee*
price	**le prix**	*luh pree*
probably	**probablement**	*probabluhmohn*
problem	**le problème**	*luh prohblehm*
pub	**le pub/le bistro**	*luh puhb/ luh beestroh*
public transport	**les transports en commun**	*lay trohnspore ohn communn*
to put	**mettre**	*mehtruh*

Q

quality	**la qualité**	*lah kaleetay*
quantity	**la quantité**	*lah konteetay*
query	**la question**	*lah kestyohn*
question	**la question**	*lah kestyohn*
queue	**la queue**	*lah kuh*
quick	**rapide**	*rapeed*
quickly	**rapidement**	*rapeeduhmohn*
quiet	**calme**	*kalm*
quite	**assez**	*assay*
quiz (school)	**l'interrogation**	*l'ahntayrogasion*
quiz (game)	**le quiz**	*luh quiz*

R

radio	la radio	*lah radyo*
railway	le chemin de fer	*luh shumahn duh fair*
rape	le viol	*luh veeyol*
ready	prêt	*prey*
real	réel	*ray-el*
receipt	le reçu	*luh ruhsu*
to receive	recevoir	*ruhsuhvwar*
reception	la réception	*lah raysepsion*
receptionist	réceptionniste	*raysepsioneest*
to recommend	recommander	*ruhkohmohnday*
reduction	la réduction	*lah raydooksion*
refund	le remboursement	*luh rohmboorsemohn*
to refuse	refuser	*ruhfoosay*
to relax	se détendre	*suh daytohndruh*
rent	le loyer	*luh lwayay*
to rent	louer	*loo-ay*
to request	demander	*duhmohnday*
reservation	la réservation	*lah raysairvasion*
to reserve	réserver	*raysairvay*
retired	à la retraite	*ah la ruhtret*
rich	riche	*reesh*
to ride	monter	*mohntay*
right	droite	*drewat*
to be right	avoir raison	*avwar raysohn*
to ring	sonner	*sonnay*
road	la route	*lah root*
to rob	voler	*volay*
room	la chambre	*lah shohmbr*
route	l'itinéraire	*l'eeteenayrair*
ruins	les ruines	*lay ruhween*

S

sauna	le sauna	*luh sohna*
Scotland	L'Ecosse	*l'aykoss*
Scottish	écossais	*aykossay*
sea	la mer	*lah mair*
seat	le siège	*luh syayzhe*
seat belt	la ceinture de sécurité	*lah sentoor duh saykooreetay*
sedative	le sédatif	*luh seydahteef*
self-service	le self-service	*luh self-sairveess*
to sell	vendre	*vohndr*
to send	envoyer	*ohnvwayay*
September	septembre	*septohmbruh*
service	le service	*luh sairveess*
shop	le magasin	*luh magasahn*
shopping	les courses	*lay koors*
shopping centre	le centre commercial	*luh sohntruh commairsyal*
show	le spectacle	*luh spectakluh*
to show	montrer	*mohntrey*
shut	fermé	*fairmey*
sign	le signe	*luh seeny*
to sign	signer	*seenyay*

sir	**monsieur**	*muh<u>syuh</u>*
sister	**la sœur**	*lah sir*
ski	**le ski**	*luh skee*
to sleep	**dormir**	*dor<u>meer</u>*
sleeping pill	**le somnifère**	*luh somnee<u>fair</u>*
to smoke	**fumer**	*fu<u>may</u>*
some	**quelques**	*<u>kelk</u>*
something	**quelquechose**	*kelkuh<u>shows</u>*
son	**le fils**	*luh feece*
south	**sud**	*sud*
South Africa	**l'Afrique du Sud**	*l'a<u>freek</u> duh sood*
South African	**sud-africain**	*sud-afree<u>kahn</u>*
Spain	**l'Espagne**	*l'es<u>panyuh</u>*
Spanish	**espagnol**	*espan<u>yol</u>*
to spell	**épeler**	*ehpuh<u>lay</u>*
sport	**le sport**	*luh spore*
stamp	**le timbre**	*luh <u>tahm</u>bruh*
to start	**commencer**	*komohn<u>say</u>*
to start (car)	**démarrer**	*daymar<u>ray</u>*

station	**la station**	*lah stas<u>syohn</u>*

Some of the major métro stations (Luxembourg is one) offer free Internet access.

sterling pound	**le livre sterling**	*luh <u>leevr</u> stair<u>ling</u>*
to stop	**s'arrêter**	*s'are<u>tay</u>*
straight	**droit**	*drewa*
street	**la rue**	*lah ru*
stress	**le stress**	*luh stress*
suitcase	**la valise**	*lah va<u>leez</u>*
sun	**le soleil**	*luh so<u>layy</u>*
sunglasses	**les lunettes de soleil**	*lay lunet duh so<u>layy</u>*
swimming pool	**la piscine**	*lah pee<u>seen</u>*
symptom	**le symptôme**	*luh samp<u>tom</u>*

T

table	**la table**	*lah tabluh*
to take	**prendre**	*<u>prohn</u>druh*
tax	**les impôts**	*layz am<u>po</u>*
tax free	**hors-taxes**	*ore-tax*
taxi	**le taxi**	*luh ta<u>xee</u>*
telephone	**le téléphone**	*luh teyley<u>fohn</u>*
television	**la télévision**	*lah teyleyvee<u>sion</u>*
tennis	**le tennis**	*luh teh<u>neess</u>*
to text	**envoyer un SMS**	*ohnvwa<u>yay</u> uhn sms*
that	**celui-là**	*suhl<u>wee</u>-lah*

theft	**le vol**	*luh vol*

In 1933, a burglar dressed in a suit of armour tried to rob a Parisian art dealer's home. The owner was awakened by the noise and quickly overcame the thief.

then	ensuite	ohn<u>sweet</u>
there	là	lah
thing	la chose	lah shows
to be thirsty	avoir soif	a<u>vwar</u> swaf
this	celui-ci	suhl<u>wee</u>-see
through	à travers	ah tra<u>vair</u>
ticket (bus)	le ticket	luh tee<u>kay</u>
ticket (cinema)	le billet	luh bee<u>yay</u>
ticket (parking)	le ticket	luh tee<u>kay</u>
ticket (shopping)	le ticket	luh tee<u>kay</u>
time (clock)	l'heure	l'err
tip (money)	le pourboire	luh pour<u>bwahr</u>
tired	fatigué	fatee<u>gay</u>
to	à	ah
today	aujourd'hui	ojoor<u>dwee</u>
toilet (to have a quick wash)	la toilette	lah twa<u>lett</u>
toilet	les toilettes	ey twalayt
toll	le péage	luh pa<u>yazh</u>
tomorrow	demain	duh<u>mahn</u>
too	aussi	oh<u>ssee</u>
tourist office	l'office de tourisme	l'off<u>eece</u> duh too<u>reesm</u>uh
town	la ville	lah veel
train	le train	luh trahn
to translate	traduire	trad<u>weer</u>
travel	le voyage	luh vwa<u>yazh</u>
travel agency	l'agence de voyage	l'a<u>zhohnce</u> duh vwa<u>yazh</u>

U

ulcer	l'ulcère	l'ool<u>sair</u>
uncomfortable	incomfortable	ancomfore<u>tabl</u>uh
to be unconscious	avoir perdu connaissance	a<u>vwar</u> pair<u>do</u> kon-ay<u>sohnce</u>
under	sous	soo
underground (tube)	le métro	luh may<u>tro</u>
to understand	comprendre	kom<u>prohnd</u>ruh
underwear	les sous-vêtements	lay soo-vet<u>mohn</u>
unemployed	au chômage	oh sho<u>mazh</u>
unpleasant	déplaisant	deyplay<u>sohn</u>
up	en haut	ohn oh
urgent	urgent	ur<u>zhon</u>
to use	utiliser	ooteelee<u>say</u>
useful	utile	oo<u>teel</u>
usually	d'habitude	d'abee<u>tud</u>

V

vacant	libre	leebr
vacation	les vacances	lay va<u>cohnce</u>
vaccination	le vaccin	luh va<u>xahn</u>
valid	valide	va<u>leed</u>
value	la valeur	lah va<u>lur</u>
valuables	les objets de valeur	layz ob<u>jay</u> duh va<u>luhr</u>
VAT	la TVA	lah tay vay ah

vegetarian **végétarien** *vayjaytar̲y̲an*
Being a vegetarian in France can be tough. Whilst the
South counts a number of vegetarian dishes, France's
cuisine is very meat-based and you might need to order
off-the-menu.

vehicle	le véhicule	*luh vayee<u>kool</u>*
very	très	*trey*
visa	le visa	*luh vee<u>za</u>*
visit	la visite	*lah vee<u>zeet</u>*
to visit	visiter	*veezee<u>tay</u>*
vitamin	la vitamine	*lah veeta<u>meen</u>*
to vomit	vomir	*voh<u>meer</u>*

W

waiter/waitress	le serveur/la serveuse	*luh sair <u>vuhr</u>/lah sair<u>vurs</u>*
waiting room	la salle d'attente	*lah sal d'at<u>tohnte</u>*
Wales	le Pays de Galles	*luh pa<u>yee</u> duh gal*
to walk	marcher	*mar<u>shay</u>*
wallet	le portefeuille	*luh portuh<u>fuy</u>*
to want	vouloir	*<u>voo</u>lwar*
to wash	laver	*la<u>vay</u>*
watch	la montre	*lah <u>mohnt</u>r*
to watch	regarder	*ruhgar<u>day</u>*
water	l'eau	*l'oh*
way (manner)	la manière	*lah manee<u>yair</u>*
way (route)	la voie	*lah vwa*

weather **le temps** *luh tohm*
Splendid weather is one of Provence's main attractions.
Besides sunshine, it also boasts wild nature and a
varied, lush vegetation.

way in	l'entrée	*l'ohn<u>trey</u>*
way out	la sortie	*lah sor<u>tee</u>*
web	le web	*luh web*
website	le site web	*luh seet web*
week	la semaine	*lah suh<u>men</u>*
weekday	le jour de la semaine	*luh zhoor duh la suhmen*
weekend	le week end	*luh wee<u>kend</u>*
welcome	bienvenue	*byenvuh<u>nu</u>*
well	bien	*byen*
Welsh	gallois	*<u>galwa</u>*
west	ouest	*west*
what?	quoi?	*kwa?*
wheelchair	la chaise roulante	*lah shays roo<u>lohnte</u>*
when?	quand?	*kohn?*
where?	où?	*oo?*
which?	lequel? laquelle?	*luh<u>kell</u>? lah<u>kell</u>?*
while	pendant que	*pohn<u>dohn</u> kuh*

who?	**qui?**	*kee?*
why?	**pourquoi?**	*poorkwa?*
wife	**la femme**	*lah fam*
wine	**le vin**	*luh vahn*
with	**avec**	*avek*
without	**sans**	*sohn*
woman	**la femme**	*lah fam*
word	**le mot**	*luh moh*
world	**le monde**	*luh mohnd*
work	**le travail**	*luh travay*
to work (person)	**travailler**	*travahyay*
to work (machine)	**marcher**	*marshay*
worried	**inquiet**	*ankyay*
to write	**écrire**	*aycreer*
wrong (mistaken)	**faux**	*foh*

X

xenophobe	**le xénophobe**	*luh zenofohb*
xenophobia	**la xénophobie**	*lah zenofohbee*
x-ray	**la radiographie**	*lah radyografee*
to x-ray	**radiographier**	*radyografeeyay*
x-rays	**des rayons x**	*dey rayohn x*

Y

yacht	**le yacht**	*yoht*
year	**l'année**	*l'annay*
yearly	**annuel**	*annu-el*
yellow pages	**les pages jaunes**	*lay pazh zhone*
yes	**oui**	*wee*
yesterday	**hier**	*eeyair*
yet	**encore**	*ohnkore*
you (formal)	**vous**	*voo*
you (informal)	**tu**	*tu*
young	**jeune**	*l'oba*
your (formal)	**votre**	*zhuhn*
your (informal)	**ton/ta**	*votruh*
youth hostel	**l'auberge de jeunesse**	*l'obairzh duh zhuhness*

Z

zebra crossing	**le passage piétons**	*luh passazh pyaytohn*
zone	**la zone**	*lah zon*
zoo	**le zoo**	*luh zo-oh*

A

à	*ah*	at/to
abîmer	*abeemay*	to damage
l'accident	*l'axeedohn*	accident
acheter	*ashuhtay*	to buy
l'addition	*ladisyohn*	bill (bar/restaurant)
l'aéroport	*l'airopore*	airport
les affaires	*leyz affair*	business
l'Afrique du Sud	*l'afreek doo sood*	South Africa
l'agence de voyage	*l'azhohnce duh vwayazh*	travel agency
aider	*ayday*	to help
aimer	*aymay*	to like
l'alarme	*l'alahrm*	alarm
l'alarme incendie	*l'alahrm ahnsohndee*	fire alarm
aller	*allay*	to go
l'allergie	*l'alairjee*	allergy
l'ambassade	*l'ohmbassad*	embassy
l'ambulance	*l'ohmboolohnce*	ambulance
américain	*amayreekahn*	American
l'Amérique	*l'amayreek*	America
l'ami/e	*l'amee*	friend
l'analgésique	*l'ahnaljayzeek*	painkiller
anglais	*ohnglay*	English
l'Angleterre	*l'ohngluhtair*	England
l'année	*l'annay*	year
l'anniversaire	*l'aneevairsair*	Anniversary
annuel	*annu-el*	yearly
annuler	*anooley*	to cancel

août	*oot*	August

August is the month for summer **fêtes** in the small villages in France – you'll see these announced on decorated signs in the village!

l'appareil photo	*l'apparey fotoh*	camera
l'appartement	*l'apartuhmohn*	apartment
appeler	*appuhlay*	to call
après	*aprey*	after
l'après soleil	*l'aprey solay*	after sun lotion
l'argent	*l'arzhohn*	money
arranger	*ahrohnjay*	to arrange
l'arrêt de bus	*l'array duh booce*	bus stop
l'arrivée	*l'ahreevey*	arrival
l'art	*l'ahr*	art
les articles de toilette	*les arteekluh duh twalett*	toiletries
l'ascenseur	*l'assohnssuhr*	lift

l'aspirine	l'aspee<u>reen</u>	aspirin
assez	a<u>ssay</u>	enough
assez	a<u>ssay</u>	quite
l'assurance	l'assoo<u>rohnce</u>	insurance
attaquer	atta<u>kay</u>	to attack
attention	attohn<u>sion</u>	attention/careful
au chômage	oh sho<u>mazh</u>	unemployed
au moins	oh mwan	at least
au secours!	oh suh<u>koor</u>!	help!
l'auberge de jeunesse	l'o<u>bairzh</u> duh zhuh-<u>ness</u>	youth hostel
aujourd'hui	ojoor<u>dwee</u>	today
aussi	oh<u>ssee</u>	too/also
l'Australie	l'ostra<u>lee</u>	Australia
australien	ostralee<u>yehn</u>	Australian
autour	o<u>toor</u>	around
autre	otr	other
un autre	uhn otr	another
avant	a<u>vohn</u>	before
avec	a<u>vek</u>	with
l'avion	l'a<u>vyohn</u>	aeroplane
l'avocat	l'ahvo<u>ka</u>	lawyer
avoir	a<u>vwar</u>	to have
avoir besoin de	a<u>vwar</u> buh<u>swan</u> duh	to need
avoir faim	a<u>vwar</u> fahm	to be hungry
avoir perdu connaissance	a<u>vwar</u> pair<u>do</u> kon-ay<u>sohnce</u>	to be unconscious
avoir raison	a<u>vwar</u> ray<u>sohn</u>	to be right
avoir soif	a<u>vwar</u> swaf	to be thirsty
avril	a<u>vreel</u>	April

B

| les bagages | lay ba<u>gazh</u> | baggage |
| le bain | luh bahn | bath |

le baiser	luh bay<u>zay</u>	kiss

A large proportion of French people still kiss on both cheeks when they greet a friend – even between men.

le bar	luh bahr	bar (pub)
en bas	ohn ba	down
beaucoup de	boh<u>koo</u> duh	much/many
le bébé	luh beh<u>beh</u>	baby
le berceau	luh bair<u>so</u>	cot
la bibliothèque	lah beebleeyo<u>tek</u>	library
bien	byen	good/well
bientôt	byen<u>toh</u>	soon
bienvenue	byenvuh<u>nu</u>	welcome
le billet	luh bee<u>yay</u>	note (money)
le billet	luh bee<u>yay</u>	ticket (cinema)

la boîte de nuit — *lah bwat duh nwee* — club/disco/nightclub
Possibly France's most famous club is Les Caves du Roy in St Tropez, which has played host to some of the glitziest parties known to mankind.

le bonnet de bain	*luh bonnay duh bahn*	bathing cap
bravo	*bravoh*	well done
brûler	*brooley*	to burn
le bureau	*luh buro*	office
le bureau de change	*luh buro duh shohnzhuh*	bureau de change
le bureau de poste	*luh buro duh pohst*	post office
le bus	*luh booce*	bus

C

la cabine d'essayage	*lah kabeen d'essayazh*	fitting room
la cabine téléphonique	*lah kabeen teyleyfohneek*	telephone box
le café	*luh kafay*	café
la calculatrice	*lah kalkulatreess*	calculator
calme	*kalm*	quiet
la campagne	*lah kampanyuh*	countryside
le carrefour	*luh karfoor*	junction
la carte	*lah kart*	map (city)
la carte	*lah kart*	map (road)
la carte d'embarquemnt	*lah kart d'ohmbarkuhmohn*	boarding card
la carte d'identité	*lah kart d'eedenteetay*	identity card
la carte de crédit	*lah kart duh kraydee*	credit card
la cartouche	*lah kartoosh*	carton (cigarettes)
le casino	*luh caseeno*	casino
la cathédrale	*lah kataydrahl*	cathedral
le CD	*luh seydey*	cd

la ceinture de sécurité — *lah sentoor duh saykooreetay* — seatbelt
Wearing a seatbelt is compulsory in France. Under – 10s must also sit in the back and either wear a seatbelt or be strapped into a child seat.

celui-ci	*suhlwee-see*	this
celui-là	*suhlwee-lah*	that
le centre	*luh sohntr*	centre
le centre commercial	*luh sohntruh commairsyal*	shopping centre
la chaise roulante	*lah shays roolohnte*	wheelchair
la chaleur	*lah shaluhr*	heat
la chambre	*lah shohmbr*	room
changer	*shohnzhay*	to change
la charge	*lah sharzhuh*	charge

chaud	*show*	hot
le chemin de fer	*luh shumahn duh fair*	railway
le chèque	*luh shek*	cheque
les cheveux	*lay shuhvuh*	hair
la chose	*lah shows*	thing
la cigare	*lah seegar*	cigar
la cigarette	*lah seegaret*	cigarette
le cinéma	*luh seenaymah*	cinema
la classe affaires	*lah klass affair*	business class
le clavier	*luh clavyay*	keyboard
la clé	*lah clay*	key
le client	*luh cleeyohn*	customer
le code postal	*luh kod postahl*	area code
combien?	*kombyen?*	how much?
la comédie musicale	*lah komaydee moozeekahl*	musical
commander	*komohnday*	to order
commencer	*komohnsay*	to start
comment?	*kommohn?*	how?
comprendre	*komprohndruh*	to understand
le conducteur	*luh kondukterr*	driver
conduire	*kondweer*	to drive
la confirmation	*lah kohnfeermasion*	confirmation
confirmer	*kohnfeermey*	to confirm
connaître	*conaytruh*	to know (person)
le consulat	*luh konsulah*	consulate
contacter	*contactey*	to contact
contagieux	*kontazhyuh*	contagious
la corrida	*lah curida*	bullfight
la côte	*lah kot*	coast
à côté de	*ah kohtay duh*	beside/next to
la couleur	*lah koolerr*	colour
couper	*koopay*	to cut
la coupure	*lah koopoor*	cut
courir	*kooreer*	to run
le courrier	*luh kooreeyay*	mail/post
les courses	*lay koors*	shopping
court	*koor*	short
le court de tennis	*luh koor duh tehneess*	tennis court
le coût	*luh koo*	cost
coûter	*kootey*	to cost
la crème	*lah krem*	cream
le crime	*luh kreem*	crime
le cyclisme	*luh seeklismuh*	cycling

D

d'accord	*dahkor*	Ok
d'habitude	*d'abeetud*	usually
la dame	*lah dam*	lady
les dames	*lay dam*	ladies (toilets)
le danger	*luh dohnzhay*	danger
dans	*dohn*	in
la date	*lah dat*	date (calendar)
de	*duh*	from/of

décembre	*daysohmbruh*	December
dehors	*duh-or*	outside
demain	*duhmahn*	tomorrow
demander	*duhmohndey*	to ask/request
démarrer	*daymarray*	To start (car)
un demi	*uhn duhmee*	half
dépêche- toi! (polite: dépêchez-vous!)	*daypesh twa! (daypeshay-voo!)*	hurry up!
déplaisant	*deyplaysohn*	unpleasant
depuis	*duhpwee*	since
déranger	*dayrohnjay*	to disturb
le dernier	*luh dairnyay*	last
derrière	*daireeyair*	behind
se déshydrater	*suh dayseedratay*	to dehydrate
le désinfectant	*luh dayzahnfectohn*	disinfectant
se détendre	*suh daytohndruh*	to relax
devoir	*duhvwar*	must
difficile	*deefeeseal*	difficult
les directions	*lay deereeksion*	directions
disponible	*deesponeebluh*	available
le distributeur automatique de billets	*luh deestreebootur automateek duh beeyay*	cash point
la distribution express	*lah deestreebusion express*	express (delivery)
donner	*donnay*	to give
dormir	*dormeer*	to sleep
la douane	*lah dwan*	customs
double	*doobluh*	double
la douche	*lah doosh*	shower
doux	*doo*	soft
la drogue	*lah drog*	drug
des drogues	*dey drog*	drugs
droit	*drewa*	straight
droite	*drewat*	right
du coin	*doo kwan*	local
du jour au lendemain	*doo zhoor oh lohnduhmahn*	overnight
du liquide	*doo leekeed*	cash
du tabac	*doo tabah*	tobacco

E

l'eau	*l'oh*	water
écossais	*aykossay*	Scottish
L'Ecosse	*l'aykoss*	Scotland
écouter	*aykootay*	to listen to
écrire	*aycreer*	to write
l'église	*l'ehgleez*	church

---

l'e-mail   *luh ee-mell*   e-mail
There are French language equivalents for most
internet-related terms but these are not used in
practice. The French use the English terms.

embrasser	ohmbra*ssay*	to kiss/hug
les employés	layz ohmpl'wa*yay*	staff
en	ahn	by (by air, car, etc)
encore	ohn*kore*	again/yet
l'endroit	l'ohn*drewa*	place
l'enfant	l'ohn*fohn*	child
enregistrer ses bagages	ahn*rezh*eestray se bah*gazh*	to check in (airport)
ensuite	ohn*sweet*	then/after that
entre	*ontruh*	between
l'entrée	l'ohn*trey*	way in
envoyer	ohnvwa*yay*	to send
envoyer un SMS	ohnvwa*yay* uhn sms	to text
épeler	ehpuh*lay*	to spell
l'erreur	l'eh*ruhrr*	error
les escaliers	layz eskalee*yay*	stairs
l'Espagne	l'es*pan*yuh	Spain
espagnol	espan*yol*	Spanish
et	eh	and
éteint	eh*tahn*	off (switched)
l'étiquette	l'ehtee*ket*	label
être	*ehtruh*	to be
exactement	exactuh*mohn*	exactly
exporter	expor*tay*	to export
l'exposition	l'exposee*sion*	exhibition
à l'extérieur	ah l'exteyree*yur*	outdoor

F

en face de	ohn fars duh	opposite (place)
faire	fair	to make
faire mal	fair mal	to hurt
faire payer	fair pa*yay*	to charge
faire un numéro	fair uhn *noo*mayro	to dial (a number)
fatigué	fatee*gay*	tired
faux	foh	wrong (mistaken)
faxer	fax*ay*	to fax
félicitations!	feyleeseetasion!	congratulations!
la femme	lah fam	woman/wife
fermé	fair*may*	closed/shut
fermer	fair*may*	to close
la fermeture éclair	lah fairmuh*tur ay*clair	zip
la fête	lah fet	party
le feu	luh fuh	fire
février	*fev*reeyay	February
la fille	*lah feey*	girl/daughter
le film	luh feelm	film (cinema)
le fils	luh feece	son
finalement	feenaluh*mohn*	at last
finir	fee*neer*	to finish
une fois	oon fwa	once
le football	luh foot*boll*	football
le formulaire	luh formoo*lair*	form (document)
frais	frey	cool
frapper	frap*pay*	to knock/hit
le frère	frair	brother

| froid | *frwa* | cold |
| fumer | *fumay* | to smoke |

G

gagner	*ganyay*	to win
la galerie	*lah galuhree*	gallery
gallois	*galwa*	Welsh
le gamin	*luh gamahn*	kid
le garage	*luh garazh*	garage
la garantie	*lah garohntee*	guarantee
le garçon	*luh garsohn*	boy
garder	*garday*	to keep
la gare routière	*lah gar rootyair*	bus station
se garer	*suh garay*	to park
gauche	*gohsh*	left
le gaz	*luh gaz*	gas
le genre	*luh zhonr*	kind (sort)
les gens	*lay zhon*	people
gentil	*zhontee*	nice (people)
le gérant	*luh zhayrohn*	manager
le gilet de sauvetage	*luh zheelay duh sohvuhtazh*	life jacket
le golf	*luh golf*	golf
grand	*grohn*	big/tall
la grande ville	*lah grohndc veel*	city
gratuit	*gratwee*	free (money)
la grippe	*lah greep*	flu
le groupe	*luh group*	group

| le guichet /la caisse | *luh geeshay /la kayss* | ticket office, box office |

Although there is a French word for box office, many people now refer to these by their English name le box office!

| le guide | *luh geed* | guide |

H

handicapé	*ohndeekapay*	disabled
en haut	*ohn oh*	up/upstairs
haut	*oh*	high
l'heure	*l'err*	time (clock)
hier	*eeyair*	yesterday
l'homme	*l'ohm*	man
homosexuel	*ohmoseksuahl*	homosexual
l'hôpital	*l'opeetal*	hospital
hors service	*ohr sairveess*	out of order
hors-taxes	*ore-tax*	tax free
l'hôtel de ville	*l'ohtel duh veel*	town hall

I

ici	*eecee*	here
il y a	*eel ee ya*	ago/there is
l'île	*l'eel*	island

immédiatement	*eemaydeeyatuh<u>mohn</u>*	immediately/at once
impoli	*ampoh<u>lee</u>*	rude
important	*ampor<u>tohn</u>*	important
importer	*ampor<u>tey</u>*	to import
les impôts	*layz am<u>po</u>*	tax
incomfortable	*ancomfore<u>tabluh</u>*	uncomfortable
information	*anforma<u>sion</u>*	information
inquiet	*an<u>kyay</u>*	worried
intéressant	*anteyrey<u>ssohn</u>*	interesting
à l'interieur	*ah l'anteyree<u>yur</u>*	Inside
international	*antairnasio<u>nal</u>*	international

l'interrogation	*l'ahntayroga<u>sion</u>*	interrogation

It is not unusual for French companies to perform graphology or handwriting analysis on job applicants.

l'intoxication alimentaire	*l'ahntoxyka<u>sion</u> ahleemohn<u>tair</u>*	food poisoning
l'Irlande	*l'ear<u>lohnde</u>*	Ireland
irlandais	*earlohn<u>day</u>*	Irish
l'itinéraire	*l'eeteenay<u>rair</u>*	itinerary/route

J

jamais	*zha<u>may</u>*	never
janvier	*zhonv<u>yay</u>*	January
le jet ski	*luh jet-skee*	jet ski
jeune	*zhuhn*	young
joli	*zhoh<u>lee</u>*	pretty
le jour	*luh zhoor*	day
le jour de la semaine	*luh zhoor duh la suh<u>men</u>*	weekday
le jour férié	*luh zhoor feyree<u>yay</u>*	holiday
le journal	*luh zhoor<u>nahl</u>*	newspaper
juillet	*jwee<u>yay</u>*	July
juin	*jwahn*	June

K

le kiosque	*luh kyosk*	kiosk

L

là	*lah*	there
laid	*lay*	ugly
la lame de rasoir	*lah lahm duh ra<u>swar</u>*	razor blade
le langage	*luh lohn<u>gazh</u>*	language
laver	*la<u>vay</u>*	to wash
la laverie automatique	*lah lav<u>ree</u> autohma<u>teek</u>*	launderette
lent	*lohn*	slow
les lentilles de contact	*lay lohn<u>tee</u> duh cohn<u>tact</u>*	contact lenses
lequel?/ laquelle?	*luh<u>kell</u>?/ lah<u>kell</u>?*	which?
lettre	*<u>lettruh</u>*	letter
libre	*leebr*	free (vacant)

le livre	*luh leevr*	book
le livre sterling	*luh leevr stairling*	sterling pound
local	*lowkahl*	local
le logement	*luh lohzhmohn*	accommodation
loin	*lwahn*	far
louer	*looayluh*	to hire/rent
le loyer	*lwayay*	rent
des lunettes	*dey loonett*	glasses (sight)
les lunettes de soleil	*lay lunet duh solayy*	sunglasses

M

madame	*madahm*	madam
le magasin	*luh magasahn*	shop
mai	*mey*	May
maintenant	*mahntuhnohn*	now
mais	*may*	but
à la maison	*ah la maysohn*	at home
le maître-nageur	*luh mehtr-nazhur*	lIfeguard
malade	*malahd*	ill
manger	*mohnzhay*	to eat
la manière	*lah maneeyair*	way (manner)

manquant *mohnkohn* missing
When you talk about a person who's missing, the word
used is **disparu**, meaning disappeared.

le manque	*luh mohnk*	shortage
manquer	*mohnkay*	to miss (a train)
le marché	*luh marshay*	market
marcher	*marshay*	to walk/ to work (machine)
le mari	*luh maree*	husband
marié	*mareeyay*	married
mars	*marce*	March
(...) me manque	*(...) muh mohnk*	to miss (a person)
le mécanicien	*luh mehkaneesyan*	mechanic
le médecin	*luh mehduhsahn*	doctor
la méduse	*lah maydooze*	jellyfish
meilleur	*meyur*	best
la mer	*lah mair*	sea
la mère	*lah mair*	mother
merveilleux	*mairvayur*	wonderful
le message	*luh meyssazh*	message
les messieurs	*maysyuh*	gents (toilets)
le métro	*luh maytro*	underground (tube)
mettre	*lay mehtruh*	to put
meublé	*muhblay*	furnished
le midi	*luh meedee*	midday
mieux	*myuh*	better
le minimum	*luh minimurm*	minimum
le minuit	*luh meenwee*	midnight
la minute	*lah meenut*	minute
moins	*mwahn*	less

le moment	*luh moh<u>mohn</u>*	moment
mon/ma/mes	*mohn/mar/may*	my
le monde	*luh mohnd*	world
la monnaie	*lah mon<u>nay</u>*	currency
monsieur	*muh<u>syuh</u>*	sir
monter	*mohn<u>tay</u>*	to ride
la montre	*lah <u>mohn</u>tr*	watch
montrer	*mohn<u>trey</u>*	to show
le mot	*luh moh*	word
la mousse à raser	*lah moosse ah ra<u>zay</u>*	shaving cream
le moustique	*luh moo<u>steek</u>*	mosquito
moyen	*mwa<u>yen</u>*	facilities

la musée   *lah moo<u>zay</u>*   museum
Paris boasts over 70 museums that house some of the best art in the world. The most famous of which being the Louvre.

N

n'importe	*nam<u>port</u>*	any
la nationalité	*lah nassyonalee<u>tay</u>*	nationality
nécessaire	*neysay<u>sair</u>*	necessary
le nettoyage à sec	*luh netwa<u>yahzh</u> ah sek*	to dry clean
le nom	*luh nohm*	name
le nom de famille	*luh nohm duh fa<u>meey</u>*	surname
le nombre	*luh <u>nohm</u>bruh*	number
nord	*nor*	north
la note	*lah not*	bill (hotel)
nouveau	*noo<u>voh</u>*	new
les informations	*ley ahnforma<u>ssyohn</u>*	news
novembre	*noh<u>vom</u>bruh*	November
la nuit	*lah nwee*	night
nulle part	*nul par*	nowhere

O

l'objet	*l'ob<u>jay</u>*	object
les objets de valeur	*layz ob<u>jay</u> duh va<u>luhr</u>*	valuables
les objets trouvés	*layz ob<u>jay</u> troo<u>vay</u>*	lost property
obtenir	*obtuh<u>neer</u>*	to get
octobre	*oc<u>tohb</u>ruh*	October
l'office de tourisme	*l'of<u>feece</u> duh too<u>reesm</u>uh*	tourist office
ok	*okay*	all right
l'opticien	*l'optee<u>syen</u>*	optician's
ou	*oo*	or
où?	*oo?*	where?
ouest	*west*	west
oui	*wee*	yes
ouvert	*oo<u>vair</u>*	open
ouvrir	*oo<u>vreer</u>*	to open
l'oxygène	*l'oxee<u>jain</u>*	oxygen

les pages jaunes	*lay pazh zhone*	yellow pages
la paire	*lah pair*	pair
la papeterie	*lah papetuhree*	stationer's
le papier à cigarettes	*luh papyay ah seegaret*	cigarette paper
le papier à écrire	*luh papyay ah aycreer*	writing paper
par	*par*	by (via)
la parapluie	*lah parapl'wee*	umbrella
le parc	*luh park*	park
parce que	*parse kuh*	because
le parcours de golf	*luh parkoor duh golf*	golf course
les parents	*lay parohn*	parents
parti	*partee*	away

partir	***parteer***	**to leave**

The expression "taking French leave" has its equivalent in French, and translates as: "running off like the English" **(filer à l'anglaise)!**

pas cher	*pah shayr*	cheap
le passage piétons	*luh passazh pyaytohn*	zebra crossing
le passeport	*luh passpore*	passport
payer	*payay*	to pay
pays	*payee*	country
le Pays de Galles	*luh payee duh gal*	Wales
le péage	*luh payazh*	toll
la pélicule	*lah peyleekul*	film (camera)
pendant	*pohndohn*	during
pendant que	*pohndohn kuh*	while
penser	*pohnsay*	to think
perdre	*pairdruh*	to lose
le père	*luh pair*	father
périmé	*payreemay*	off (food)
le permis de conduire	*luh pairmee duh kondweer*	driving licence
la personne	*lah pairsohn*	person
petit	*puhtee*	small
un petit peu	*uhn puhtee puh*	little (a little)
un peu	*uhn puh*	bit (a)
peut-être	*puht-ehtruh*	maybe/perhaps
la photo	*lah fotoh*	photo
la piqûre de moustique	*lah peekoor duh moosteek*	mosquito bite
pire	*pier*	worse
la piscine	*lah peeseen*	swimming pool
la place de parking	*lah plass duh par-keeng*	parking space
la plage	*lah plazh*	beach
la plage nudiste	*lah plazh nudeest*	nudist beach
se plaindre	*suh plahndruh*	to complain
la plainte	*lah plantuh*	complaint

la pluie	*lah pl'wee*	rain
la plupart (de)	*la ploopar (duh)*	most (of)
plus	*pluce*	more
à plus tard	*ah ploo tar*	see you later
la police	*lah poleece*	police
le port	*luh pore*	port (sea)
le porte-clé	*luh portuh-clay*	key ring
le portefeuille	*luh portuhfuy*	wallet
le porto	*luh poretoh*	port (drink)
possible	*posseebluh*	possible
la poste aérienne	*lah pohst ah-air-ryen*	airmail
pour	*poor*	for

| **le pourboire** | *luh pourbwahr* | tip (money) |

The tip is very often included in restaurant and bar bills, check for the phrase **sce compris** on your bill – this means your tip has already been included!

pourquoi?	*poorkwa?*	why?
pouvoir	*poovwar*	can (to be able)
préféré	*prayfayray*	favourite
préférer	*preyfeyray*	to prefer
les premiers secours	*lay pruhmyay suhkoor*	first aid
prendre	*prohndruh*	to take
prendre plaisir à	*prohndruh playzeer ah*	to enjoy
près	*prey*	close
près de	*prey duh*	by (beside)/near
la prescription	*lah prescreepsion*	prescription
se présenter	*suh praysohntay*	to check in (hotel)
prêt	*prey*	ready
principal	*pranseepahl*	main
privé	*preevay*	private
le prix	*luh pree*	price
probablement	*probabluhmohn*	probably
le problème	*luh prohblehm*	problem
prochain	*prohshahn*	next
à propos de	*ah prohpoh duh*	about (concerning)
le propriétaire	*luh propreeyaytair*	owner
le pub/le bistro	*luh puhb/luh beestroh*	pub

Q

le quai	*leh kay*	platform
la qualité	*lah kaleetay*	quality
quand?	*kohn?*	when?
la quantité	*lah konteetay*	quantity
un quart	*uhn kar*	quarter
à quelle distance?	*ah kel deestohnce?*	how far?
quelle longueur?	*kel longuhr?*	how long?
quelle taille?	*kel tie?*	how big?
quelquechose	*kelkuhshows*	something
quelques	*kelk*	some

la question	*lah kestyohn*	query/question
la queue	*lah kuh*	queue
qui?	*kee?*	who?
le quiz	*luh quiz*	quiz (game)
quoi?	*kwa?*	what?

R

le raccourci	*luh rakoorsee*	short cut
la radio	*lah radyo*	radio
la radiographie	*lah radyografee*	x-ray
radiographier	*radyografeeyay*	to x-ray
des rayons x	*dey rayohn x*	x-rays
rapide	*rapeed*	fast/quick
rapidement	*rapeeduhmohn*	quickly
la réception	*lah raysepsion*	reception
réceptionniste	*raysepsioneest*	receptionist
recevoir	*ruhsuhvwar*	to receive
recommander	*ruhkohmohnday*	to recommend
le reçu	*luh ruhsu*	receipt
la réduction	*lah raydooksion*	discount/reduction
réel	*ray-el*	real
refuser	*ruhfoosay*	to refuse
regarder	*ruhgarday*	to look/watch
la région	*lah rayzhion*	area
le remboursement	*luh rohmboorsemohn*	refund
rencontrer	*rohnkontrey*	to meet
le rendez-vous	*luh rohnday-voo*	appointment
répondre	*reypohndr*	to answer
la réservation	*lah raysairvasion*	reservation/booking
réserver	*raysairvay*	to reserve/book
le retard	*luh retar*	delay
en retard	*ohn ruhtar*	late (time)
retardé	*ruhtarday*	late (delayed)
retour	*ruhtoor*	back (place)
à la retraite	*ah la ruhtret*	retired
la réunion	*lah rayuniohn*	meeting

rich	*riche*	rich

France is the world leader in the production of luxury goods, where the owners of companies like LVMH (which owns Louis Vuitton) and Hermès top France's rich list year after year.

rien	*ryahn*	nothing
la route	*lah root*	road
la route principale	*lah root pranseepahl*	main road
la rue	*lah ru*	street
la rue principale	*lah roo prahnseepahl*	high street
les ruines	*lay ruhween*	ruins

S

s'arrêter	*s'aretay*	to stop
sale	*sal*	dirty
la salle à manger	*lah sal ah mohnzhay*	dining room

la salle d'attente	*lah sal d'attohnte*	waiting room
le salon de coiffure	*luh salohn duh kwafoor*	hairdresser's
sans	*sohn*	without
le sauna	*luh sohna*	sauna
savoir	*savwar*	to know (knowledge)
en sécurité	*ohn saykooreetay*	safe
le sédatif	*luh seydahteef*	sedative
le self-service	*luh self-sairveess*	self-service
la semaine	*lah suhmen*	week
sensé	*sohnsey*	sensible
septembre	*septohmbruh*	September
le serveur/la serveuse	*luh sairvuhr/lah sairvurs*	waiter/waitress
le service	*luh sairveess*	service
le service des urgences	*luh sairveess deyz oorzhonce*	A&E
la serviette hygiénique	*lah sairveeyet eezhayneek*	sanitary towel
servir	*sairveer*	to serve
seulement	*suluhmohn*	just (only)
le SIDA	*luh seeda*	AIDS
le siège	*luh syayzhe*	seat
la signature	*lah seenyatur*	signature
le signe	*luh seeny*	sign
signer	*seenyay*	to sign
le site web	*luh seet web*	website

| **le ski** | *luh skee* | **ski** |
| | France boasts the highest mountain in Western Europe, Mont Blanc, which reaches over 15,000 feet. | |

---

la sœur	*lah sir*	sister
ce soir	*suh swar*	tonight
le soleil	*luh solayy*	sun
le somnifère	*luh somneefair*	sleeping pill
sonner	*sonnay*	to ring
la sortie	*lah sortee*	way out
la sortie de secours	*lah sortee duh suhkoor*	fire exit
soudainement	*soodenuhmohn*	suddenly
sous	*soo*	below/under
les sous-vêtements	*lay soo-vetmohn*	underwear
le spectacle	*luh spectakluh*	show
le sport	*luh spore*	sport
les sports nautiques	*lay spore nohteek*	water sports
le stade	*luh stad*	stadium
la station	*lah stassyohn*	station
la station de taxis	*lah stassiohn duh taxee*	taxi rank
la station-service	*lah stasiohn-sairveess*	filling (station)
le stress	*luh stress*	stress
sud	*sud*	south
sud-africain	*sud-afreekahn*	South African

sur	*suhr*	on
sympa	*sahmpa*	kind (nice)
le symptôme	*luh samp<u>tom</u>*	symptom

T

le tabac	*luh ta<u>bah</u>*	tobacconist
la table	*lah tabluh*	table
les horaires	*lay 'zo<u>rair</u>*	timetable
la tache	*lah tash*	stain
les tampons	*lay tom<u>pohn</u>*	tampons
le taux d'échange	*luh toh d'ay<u>shohnje</u>*	exchange rate
les taxes	*lay tax*	duty (tax)
le taxi	*luh ta<u>xee</u>*	taxi/cab
la teinturerie	*lah tahntooruh<u>ree</u>*	dry cleaner's
le téléphone	*luh teyley<u>fohn</u>*	phone/telephone
le téléphone mobile	*luh teyley<u>fon</u> moh<u>beel</u>*	mobile phone
téléphoner	*teyleyfoh<u>nay</u>*	to phone
la télévision	*lah teyleyvee<u>sion</u>*	television
le temps	*luh tohm*	weather
le tennis	*luh teh<u>neess</u>*	tennis
la terrasse	*lah te<u>rass</u>*	terrace
le ticket	*luh tee<u>kay</u>*	ticket (bus/parking/ shopping)
le timbre	*luh <u>tahm</u>bruh*	stamp
tissu	*tee<u>ssoo</u>*	material (cloth)
la toilette	*lah twa<u>lett</u>*	toilet (to freshen up)
les toilettes	*<u>ley</u> twa<u>layt</u>*	toilets
ton/ta	*tohn/tah*	your (informal)
tôt	*toh*	early
tout	*tooh*	all
tout droit	*too drewa*	straight ahead
traduire	*tra<u>dweer</u>*	to translate
le train	*luh trahn*	train
le train rapide	*luh trahn ra<u>peed</u>*	express (train)
le tramway	*luh trahm<u>way</u>*	tram
les transports en commun	*lay trohn<u>spore</u> ohn com<u>muhn</u>*	public transport
le travail	*luh tra<u>vayu</u>*	work
travailler	*travah<u>yay</u>*	to work (person)
à travers	*ah tra<u>vair</u>*	through
très	*trey*	very
triste	*treest*	sad
tu	*tu*	you (informal)
tuer	*toohey*	to kill
la TVA	*tuh-ehlah tay va*	VAT
typique	*tee<u>pee</u>*	typical

U

l'ulcère	*l'ool<u>sair</u>*	ulcer
un/une	*uhn/oon*	a(n)
l'urgence	*l'oor<u>johnse</u>*	emergency
urgent	*ur<u>zhon</u>*	urgent
utile	*oo<u>teel</u>*	useful
utiliser	*ooteelee<u>say</u>*	to use

V

les vacances	*lay vacohnce*	vacation/holidays
le vaccin	*luh vaxahn*	vaccination
la valeur	*lah valur*	value
valide	*valeed*	valid
la valise	*lah valeez*	suitcase
végétarien	*vayjaytaryan*	vegetarian
le véhicule	*luh vayeekool*	vehicle
le vélo	*luh veyloh*	bicycle
vendre	*vohndr*	to sell
venir	*vuhneer*	to come
les vêtements	*lay vetmohn*	clothes
la ville	*lah veel*	town
le vin	*luh vahn*	wine
le viol	*luh veeyol*	rape
le visa	*luh veeza*	visa
la visite	*lah veezeet*	visit
visiter	*veezeetay*	to visit
la vitamine	*lah veetameen*	vitamin
la vitesse	*lah veetess*	speed
la voie	*lah vwa*	way (route)
le voilier	*luh vwaleeyay*	sailing boat
la voiture	*lah vwatoor*	car
le vol	*luh vol*	flight
le vol	*luh vol*	theft
voler	*volay*	to rob
vomir	*vohmeer*	to vomit
votre	*votruh*	your (formal)
vouloir	*voolwar*	to want
vous	*voo*	you (formal)
le voyage	*luh vwayazh*	journey/travel
vrai	*vray*	true

W

| le web | *luh web* | web |
| le week end | *luh weekend* | weekend |

X

| le xénophobe | *luh zenofohb* | xenophobe |
| la xénophobie | *lah zenofohbee* | xenophobia |

Y

| le yacht | *luh yoht* | yacht |

Z

zéro	*zairo*	zero
la zone	*lah zon*	zone
le zoo	*luh zo-oh*	zoo

Quick reference

Numbers

0	zéro	_zay_ro
1	un	uhn
2	deux	duh
3	trois	trewa
4	quatre	katruh
5	cinq	sank
6	six	seess
7	sept	set
8	huit	weet
9	neuf	nerf
10	dix	deess
11	onze	ohnz
12	douze	dooz
13	treize	treyz
14	quatorze	ka_torz_
15	quinze	kanz
16	seize	sez
17	dix-sept	deess-set
18	dix-huit	deess-weet
19	dix-neuf	deess-nerf
20	vingt	van
21	vingt-et-un	vant-ay-_uhn_
30	trente	trohnt
40	quarante	ka_rohnt_
50	cinquante	san_kohnt_
60	soixante	swas_sohnt_
70	soixante-dix	swassont-_deess_
80	quatre-vingt	katruh-_van_
90	quatre-vingt-dix	katruh-van-_deess_
100	cent	sohn
1000	mille	meel
1st	premier/première	pruhm_yay_/pruhm_yair_
2nd	deuxième	duh_zyem_
3rd	troisième	trewa_zyem_
4th	quatrième	katree_yem_
5th	cinquième	sankee_yem_

Weights & measures

English	French	Pronunciation
gram (=0.03oz)	**gramme**	*gram*
kilogram (=2.2lb)	**kilogramme**	*keelogram*
centimetre (=0.4in)	**centimètre**	*sohnteemettruh*
metre (=1.1yd)	**mètre**	*mettruh*
kilometre (=0.6m)	**kilomètre**	*keelomettruh*
litre (=2.1pt)	**litre**	*leetruh*

Days & time

English	French	Pronunciation
Monday	**lundi**	*luhndee*
Tuesday	**mardi**	*mardee*
Wednesday	**mercredi**	*mairkruhdee*
Thursday	**jeudi**	*zhuhdee*
Friday	**vendredi**	*vohndruhdee*
Saturday	**samedi**	*samdee*
Sunday	**dimanche**	*deemohnshe*

What time is it?	**Quelle heure est-il?**	*kel err ay teel?*
(Four) o'clock	**(Quatre) heures**	*(katruh) err*
Quarter past (six)	**(Six) heures et quart**	*(siz) err ay kar*
Half past (eight)	**(Huit) heures et demie**	*(weet) err ay duh-mee*
Quarter to (ten)	**(Dix) heures moins le quart**	*(diz) err mwan luh kar*
morning	**matin**	*matahn*
afternoon	**après-midi**	*aprey-meedee*
evening	**soir**	*swar*
night	**nuit**	*nwee*

Clothes size converter

Women's clothes	34	36	38	40	42	44	46	50
equiv. UK size	6	8	10	12	14	16	18	20

Men's jackets	44	46	48	50	52	54	56	58
equiv. UK size	34	36	38	40	42	44	46	48

Men's shirts	36	37	38	39	40	41	42	43
equiv. UK size	14	14.5	15	15.5	16	16.5	17	17.5

Shoes	36.5	37.5	39	40	41.5	42.5	44	45
equiv. UK size	4	5	6	7	8	9	10	11